A CHAPTER GUIDE TO GENE WOLFE'S LATRO NOVELS

Michael Andre-Driussi

Sirius Fiction

Copyright © 2020 Michael Andre-Driussi

All rights reserved

No part of this book may be reproduced, or stored in a retrieval system, or transmitted in any form or by any means, electronic, mechanical, photocopying, recording, or otherwise, without express written permission of the publisher.

ISBN-13: 978-1-947614-19-2 (paperback)
ISBN-13: 978-1-947614-20-8 (ebook)

*Dedicated to those who favor Latro,
including those who have passed away.
Alice K. Turner: She puzzled, she pondered, she pounced. Only now do I catch up.
Jay André: Well-versed in both Robert Graves and Conan the Barbarian, his favorite Wolfe hero was Latro.*

CONTENTS

Title Page
Copyright
Dedication
Introduction
Soldier of the Mist 1
Appendices to Soldier of the Mist 59
Soldier of Arete 77
Appendices for Soldier of Arete 126
Soldier of Sidon 143
Appendices for Soldier of Sidon 187
Bibliography 201
Books By This Author 203

INTRODUCTION

This work is a chapter-by-chapter reading guide to Gene Wolfe's "Latro" novels: *Soldier of the Mist* (1986), *Soldier of Arete* (1989), and *Soldier of Sidon* (2006).

The Guide is intended to be used by first time readers of each book as well as those who are rereading them. The idea is that we are reading it together, you and I. There are no spoilers, but things will be noted as they are revealed.

How To Use The Guide

A reader could read a chapter of the source text first, then check in this book for the notes.

Or

A reader could read this book directly.

❖ ❖ ❖

Wolf in the OED

Using the brute force method, here are some applications of

"wolf" to watch for, from the *Oxford English Dictionary:*

wolf-spider

wolf-moth

wolf tree (this is normally a tree that dominates an area)

wolf (slang): sexually aggressive male; homosexual predator

wolf disease: lupus

wolf: an ancient military engine, used for grasping battering-rams used by besiegers

wolf: a kind of fishing net

"a hair of the same wolf" (identical to "hair of the dog that bit you")

"a wolf in sheep's clothing"

to throw to the wolves

wolf-berry: a North American shrub

wolf-fly

Wolfland: former name for Ireland

wolf pen: strong box made of logs, used for trapping wolves

wolf-stone

wolf-thistle

wolf-tick

wolf-willow

wolf's-claw: clubmoss

wolf's-tooth: farriery term for a tooth of a horse, the first grinding tooth of the upper jaw

SOLDIER OF THE MIST

Soldier Of The Mist

Edition cited: Tor (hb), ISBN 93734-2, November 1986, 335pp.

Dedication:

This book is
dedicated
with the greatest respect and affection
to
Herodotos of Halicarnassos

Commentary: Herodotus (c. 484–c. 425 BC) was an ancient Greek historian born in Halicarnassus in the Persian Empire. He wrote *The Histories* about the Greco-Persian Wars.

Epigraph:

> First there was a struggle at the barricade of shields; then, the barricade down, a bitter and protracted fight, hand to hand, at the temple of Demeter....
>
> —Herodotos

This quote is from *The Histories* (Book IX, 62). It describes the Battle of Plataea, the final land battle during the second Persian invasion of Greece, in 479 BC near the city Plataea in Boeotia.

Notes: "Although this book is fiction, it is based on actual events of 479 BC."

Foreword: (xi–xiv) How Gene Wolfe came to look over some ancient scrolls, and a few paragraphs about the culture Latro wrote about.
- Coinage
- Wages
- Homer
- The runner who saw the god Pan

Part I

Chapter I: Read This Each Day

1.01: (3–5) Latro at the healer's tent writes down the events. The healer says he spoke to Latro the day before, and he has spoken to him several times, so it is perhaps three days after the battle that took Latro's memory. Latro seems to have been in the Persian army.

The healer comes again and tells Latro he was wounded near the shrine of the Earth Mother.

Latro helps take down the tent. The large group moves out.

Persian Detail: Latro sees a soldier in fancy armor who bears a "spear with an apple of gold" (4). This identifies the man as one of the Immortals, elite soldiers.

1.02: (5–6) Latro is beside a river. The army of the Great King is so enormous he cannot imagine how it was vanquished. A black man becomes his friend, but Latro is distracted by a man under the water.

Commentary: The black man, through gestures, seems to suggest that Latro has pale skin and red hair.

1.03: (6–7) It is evening, and Latro is fading, pursued by the slaves of the Rope Makers.

Geography: "Rope Makers" are Spartans; "slaves of the Rope Makers" are helots.

1.04: (7) It is night. Latro goes to the river to talk to the god there. The god enchants his sword.

Commentary: It seems they followed the river.

Chapter II: At Hill

2.01: (8–9) Latro, after an unspecified break, writes at a new location he calls "Hill." Hill sided with the Great King in the war, and now they feel vulnerable since their best soldiers, the Sacred Band, have been killed.

Latro cannot find the healer. The black man steals food for

them both.

Geography: Hill is Thebes.

History: The Sacred Band of Thebes is provocatively anachronistic here, because in later generations there existed a military group of this name that is famous for being made up of 150 homosexual pairs.

Herodotus writes that the Athenians killed a group of 300 Theban elite at Plataea, but he does not call the Thebans "Sacred Band," nor does he mention a homosexual nature to the unit.

The theory of homosexual military groups was discussed in Plato's *Symposium* and Xenophon's *Symposium,* but these texts were written in later generations. Modern historians believe that the homosexual Sacred Band was formed in 371 BC, about a hundred years after the Battle of Plataea, and was destroyed in 338 BC.

2.02: (9–12) After they eat, Latro sees a fountain with a statue of the Swift God and calls out to him. Bystanders call out personal questions and pay for the answers Latro gives. Then men from the House of the Sun come and take them to the temple.

To resolve an argument over payment, one man donates his little slave girl, a literate virgin. The priest tests the girl's literacy, and she passes with surprising skill.

Latro sees a golden man, a god who speaks to him of the Unknown God, and then gives direct prophecy about Latro's future. Latro does not hear what the pythoness says.

Latro writes at the temple of the Shining God.

Myth: The Swift God, the river god who had blessed Latro's sword, remains unnamed; the temple of the Shining God sounds like the Temple of Apollo Ismenios: the god tells Latro "I am the slayer of wolves" (11) and he speaks of Latro's headwound as bearing a wolf's tooth (12).

Bible: When Apollo mentions "the Unknown God," this is an unexpected echo to an episode in the New Testament when Paul visited Athens and found a shrine to the Unknown God:

And they took him, and brought him unto Areopagus, saying, May we know what this new doctrine, whereof thou speakest, is?

For thou bringest certain strange things to our ears: we would know therefore what these things mean.

(For all the Athenians and strangers which were there spent their time in nothing else, but either to tell, or to hear some new thing.)

Then Paul stood in the midst of Mars' hill, and said, Ye men of Athens, I perceive that in all things ye are too superstitious.

For as I passed by, and beheld your devotions, I found an altar with this inscription, To The Unknown God. Whom therefore ye ignorantly worship, him declare I unto you.

God that made the world and all things therein, seeing that he is Lord of heaven and earth, dwelleth not in temples made with hands;

Neither is worshipped with men's hands, as though he needed any thing, seeing he giveth to all life, and breath, and all things;

And hath made of one blood all nations of men for to dwell on all the face of the earth, and hath determined the times before appointed, and the bounds of their habitation;

That they should seek the Lord, if haply they might feel after him, and find him, though he be not far from every one of us:

For in him we live, and move, and have our being; as certain also of your own poets have said, For we are also his offspring.

Forasmuch then as we are the offspring of God, we ought not to think that the Godhead is like unto gold, or silver, or stone, graven by art and man's device.

And the times of this ignorance God winked at; but now commandeth all men every where to repent:

Because he hath appointed a day, in the which he will judge the world in righteousness by that man whom he hath ordained; whereof he hath given assurance unto all men, in that he hath raised him from the dead.

And when they heard of the resurrection of the dead,

some mocked: and others said, We will hear thee again of this matter.

So Paul departed from among them. (Acts 17:19–33)

Chapter III: Io

3.01: (13–19) Latro wakes back in the military camp. He meets his new slave girl Io and the poet Pindaros.

The poet says the army is being led by Artabazus. Pindaros has little Io recite what the pythoness said the day before and offers his interpretation, ending with his reason why they are now heading to Lebadeia.

As dawn comes to the lake, a large party of the Kid begins, and Latro's group is drawn to participate, leaving the army behind.

History: Pindaros mentions Mardonius as the Persian army leader, states that he is dead, and says that Artabazus is now in charge. History agrees that Mardonius was killed at Plataea, so this army is the remnant that Artabazus led back to the Empire, and it stopped at Thebes as a friendly "port."

Pindaros: Pindaros, in English known as "Pindar," was a famous lyric poet of ancient Greece. In 479 BC he was nearly forty years old and in the middle of his career, but there are no known poems of his from that year.

In the novel, Latro says, "I feel I've been dreaming and have just awakened; but I can't tell you what my dream was, or what preceded it," a line that Pindaros writes down (14). It looks something like a bit from a Pindaros poem: "Things of a day—what are we, and what not? Man is a dream of shadows" ("Pythian VIII, For Aristomeses").

Onomastics: Io means "joy."

Myth: The Kid is Dionysus, god of wine. Io is named after a Greek princess who was one of the mortal lovers of Zeus. He turned her into a heifer, but his wife took the heifer as a pet and set Argus to watch it.

Geography: The lake is Copais, a body of water drained in the 19th century.

Lebadeia, about 45 km/27 mi west of Thebes, was famous for having an oracular cavern one descended into. This is probably what Pindaros is aiming for. "*Trophonius's Cave*—One of the many entrances to the Land of the Dead" (*Mist* glossary).

Chapter IV: Awakened by Moonlight

4.01: (20–27) Latro wakes, naked in the grass beside a nude woman. He goes to the water to wash. He sees the virgin goddess with bow and arrows. The sun rises.

The woman is violet-eyed Hilaeira.

The priest tells young Io "there are many gods, but not so many as ignorant people suppose" (22). He says Great Mother, Earth Mother, and Pig Lady are the same. He tells her about his god the Kid, who is also known as the God of the Tree and the King from Nysa. The Descender impregnated Semele, princess of Hill, but his wife Teleia learned and tricked the girl into having her lover reveal his divinity. The Lady of Thought, a goddess, played both sides of the marital spat. The priest ends with saying that the drunken orgy the night before was a celebration about the Kid going through that lake to rescue his mother from the underworld.

Latro's group is heading for Lebadeia to visit the Great Mother shrine there. They stop at a house to eat. Swarthy men come over the hill.

Myth: The virgin goddess with bow and arrows sounds like Artemis.

The Kid, Dionysus, is also known as the God of the Tree and the King from Nysa. Making the familiar into strange, the Descender is Zeus; Teleia is a title of Hera as goddess of marriage. That the Kid went to Hades to rescue his mother is a curious parallel to the more famous case of Orpheus who went to Hades to rescue his wife. The priest tells Latro that Lake Copais is an entryway to the underworld, one used by Dionysus; this sounds like the claim made for Lake Lerna, located south of Argos.

The Lady of Thought is Athena.

Onomastics: Hilaeira means "brightness" (*Mist* glossary).

Chapter V: Among the Slaves of the Rope Makers

5.01: (28–34) Latro's group is taken prisoner.

They are marching along, being beaten. Latro sees an old black man sleeping near the road. He says he is the King of Nysa, rewarded by his pupil the Kid. He plays the flute and Latro sings.

They don't beat Latro after that.

Pindaros tells Latro that he has completed two lines of the prophetic verse.

A sentry takes Latro's scroll. Latro speaks to a serpent woman, who follows the sentry and returns with the scroll. She says she drank from the sentry.

Pindaros tells Latro about kingship originating with the gods and their children.

Pindaros: The poet says, "The ages to come are wisest" (34), which shows some faint echo of "the days that follow after are the wisest witnesses" ("Olympian I").

Myth: The Thunderer is Zeus; the Twice-Born God is Dionysus.

Commentary: The group had some safety when with the retreating army, but they were quickly picked off when they left the main body.

Chapter VI: Eos

6.01: (35–42) Latro sleeps a little before being awakened in the night by Cerdon, one of the captors. He says the old black man was a god. The serpent woman hisses, but Latro will not let her have Cerdon.

Cerdon tells how the Slaves of the Rope Makers used to be free, and how they worshipped the Great Mother. Then the Rope Makers came along with their god the Descender.

The serpent woman is a daughter of Enodia.

Pindaros recites some poetry. Latro asks him about snake women. Pindaros says Heracles supposedly killed them all in that area.

Io confesses that she lied when she said the Bright God gave her to Latro.

The next morning Latro sees the lady of the dawn and she traces her name on his scroll.

Myth: The Lady of the Dawn is Eos; the Great Mother is Demeter; the Descender is Zeus; and Enodia is Hecate (the Dark Moon goddess, in distinction from the Crescent Moon goddess and the Full Moon goddess). That Heracles killed snake-women is difficult to find, unless it is a version of the Stymphalian Birds.

The old black man is Silenus, a teacher of the Kid (Dionysus). He seems to be a black man like Latro's soldier friend, and this seems to reinforce the Ethiopian location of "Nysa" as implied when the priest saw Latro's friend. The Homeric Hymn "To Dionysus" begins with this:

> (ll. 1-9) For some say, at Dracanum; and some, on windy Icarus; and some, in Naxos, O Heaven-born, Insewn; and others by the deep-eddying river Alpheus that pregnant Semele bare you to Zeus the thunder-lover. And others yet, lord, say you were born in Thebes; but all these lie. The Father of men and gods gave you birth remote from men and secretly from white-armed Hera. There is a certain Nysa, a mountain most high and richly grown with woods, far off in Phoenice, near the streams of Aegyptus.

Onomastics: Jeremy Crampton decodes "Cerdon" as meaning "Cunning Conman." Commentary upon Herodas's "Mime 6" and "Mime 7" verify this, stating that Cerdon, normally a slave name, means "moneymaker" or "profiteer."

Pindaros: When Pindaros says, "Arrows have I for the hearts of the wise..." (40), he is quoting a bit of "Olympian II."

Herodotus: The historian in Book VI tells of a chance meeting between a man and a god around this time (an incident summarized at the end of Wolfe's foreword) that bears some similarity to Latro's situation:

> 105. First of all, while they were still in the city, the generals sent off to Sparta a herald, namely Pheidippides an Athenian and for the rest a runner of long day-courses and

one who practised this as his profession. With this man, as Pheidippides himself said and as he made report to the Athenians, Pan chanced to meet by mount Parthenion, which is above Tegea; and calling aloud the name of Pheidippides, Pan bade him report to the Athenians and ask for what reason they had no care of him, though he was well disposed to the Athenians and had been serviceable to them on many occasions before that time, and would be so also yet again. Believing that this tale was true, the Athenians, when their affairs had been now prosperously settled, established under the Acropolis a temple of Pan; and in consequence of this message they propitiate him with sacrifice offered every year and with a torch-race.

The civic reaction also reflects upon Pindaros's earlier statement that "a committee of our citizens has chosen me to guide [Latro]" (26).

End of Part I

Synopsis of Part I: From Clay to the Lady of Dawn (chapters I to VI)

Latro's new memory problem. The prophetic verses. The slave girl Io is given to Latro. The poet Pindaros joins the group. The woman Hilaeira joins the group. The group is enslaved by Rope Maker slaves. Latro meets Silenus. A serpent woman begins helping Latro.

Part II

Chapter VII: Beside the Beached Ships

7.01: (45–52) Latro wakes up in a tent on a beach, location unknown. The black man is carving a doll.

Hypereides introduces himself as Latro's new master. His three warships are *Europa, Eidyia,* and *Clytia.*

Latro's group has been with Hypereides for at least a day. Hypereides told him of Fennel Field the day before and now tells about the Battle of Peace.

Their guard is Lyson. Latro homeland hint: Where horsemen are put in charge of warships.

Onomastics: Europa was a Phoenician princess whom Zeus kidnapped in the form of a bull; Eidyia was an ocean nymph from the eastern end of the Black Sea; Clytia was a water nymph who loved Helios in vain.

Geography: Fennel Field is Marathon; Peace is Salamis.

Satyricon: The fragmented, episodic nature of Latro's narrative bears a surprising similarity to Petronius's *Satyricon,* an ancient Roman picaresque which is fragmented for having lost sections. Not only are random sections missing, but even the beginning is lost, which further matches Latro's situation.

Satyricon also has a poet as a travelling companion, analogous to Pindaros; he is Eumolpus, a character who spouts a poem on the Civil War between Julius Caesar and Pompey that goes on for five chapters.

Mystery: Latro's group was previously going west from Thebes, but then was being marched south, yet now he and his black friend seem to be on a beach between Cape Malea and Tower Hill (Corinth).

Chapter VIII: At Sea

8.01: (53–60) Another day finds Latro on the sailing *Europa*. Redface Island is on their left. Hypereides tells him about the Battle of Peace. The sail of *Europa* shows a bull with a woman on his back, and she has red hair and blue eyes. The foreign bowman wants a favor from Latro.

Latro meets with his group. Pindaros writes "Read This Each Day" on the cover of Latro's scroll. Little Io says that the black man paid out all his money for the three slaves Latro killed back when they were taken. Pindaros says the group was taken to Tower Hill, where his ten owls were confiscated, and he tells of the rivalry between the cities Thought and Tower Hill.

Latro writes on the *Europa.*

Geography: Thought is Athens; Tower Hill is Corinth.

Chapter IX: Night Comes

9.01: (61–67) The ship lands on a beach near Teuthrone. Little Io admits to Latro that she was raped by the slaves of the Rope Makers, as was Hilaeira. Then the slaves of the Rope Makers had been met by soldiers who took possession of Latro's group. The soldiers transferred them to Hypereides.

The foreign bowman introduces himself to Latro as Oior. They arrange to meet on the ridge after eating, and that is where Latro writes as it grows dark.

Geography: Teuthrone is on the western side of the Laconian Gulf. The ship seems to be coming around the island in a counterclockwise direction from Tower Hill (Corinth), and is about halfway.

Onomastics: According to Herodotus, "Oior" is Scythian for "man" (Book IV, 110).

Chapter X: Under a Waning Moon

10.01: (68–76) Little Io brings food and wine to Latro. He is approached by a woman wearing a snakeskin around her waist. He tells Io to go to the fire. The woman says the crescent moon is a goddess. She says one will die, then she vanishes.

Oior comes along. He tells Latro that his land from the Ister to the Island Sea was once ruled by the Sons of Cimmer, who sacrificed their sons to Artimpasa (the Triple Goddess). They mistakenly sacrificed an acolyte of Apia (the Great Mother), for which the king, the acolyte's father, wanted them killed. The sorcerers fled and became the Neuri, but they imitate the Sons of Scoloti to avoid detection. The Neuri are cursed by the Great Mother to turn into a wolf once a year.

Oior says there is such a werewolf on the ship, one of the other three bowmen. He asks Latro to look each in the eye. As they start walking, Latro is taken by the neck.

Geography: The Ister "A great river emptying into the Euxine" (*Mist* glossary), probably the Danube; the Island Sea "A landlocked sea east of the Euxine" (*Mist* glossary) is presumably the Caspian Sea.

Herodotus: The historian tells about the "Sons of Cimmer" (Kimerians) and the Neurians in Book IV. First the Kimerians, who were displaced by the Sons of Scoloti (Scythians):

> 11. There is however also another story, which is as follows, and to this I am most inclined myself. It is to the effect that the nomad Scythians dwelling in Asia, being hard pressed in war by the Massagetai, left their abode and crossing the river Araxes came towards the Kimmerian land (for the land which now is occupied by the Scythians is said to have been in former times the land of the Kimmerians); and the Kimmerians, when the Scythians were coming against them, took counsel together, seeing that a great host was coming to fight against them; and it proved that their opinions were divided, both opinions being vehemently maintained, but the better being that of their kings: for the opinion of the people was that it was necessary to depart and that they ought not to run the risk of fighting against so many, but that of the kings was to fight for their land with those who came against them: and as neither the people were willing by means to agree to the counsel of the kings nor the kings to that of the people, the people planned to depart without fighting and to deliver up the land to the invaders, while the kings resolved to die and to be laid in their own land, and not to flee with the mass of the people, considering the many goods of fortune which they had enjoyed, and the many evils which it might be supposed would come upon them, if they fled

from their native land. Having resolved upon this, they parted into two bodies, and making their numbers equal they fought with one another: and when these had all been killed by one another's hands, then the people of the Kimmerians buried them by the bank of the river Tyras (where their burial-place is still to be seen), and having buried them, then they made their way out from the land, and the Scythians when they came upon it found the land deserted of its inhabitants.

Next, the neighboring tribe of the Neurians (as "Neuroi") in Book IV, on the other side of the Dniester river (or the "Tyras") flowing from Eastern Europe into the Black Sea:

> 51. One, I say, of the rivers which the Scythians have is the Ister; and after it the Tyras, which starts from the North and begins its course from a large lake which is the boundary between the land of the Scythians and that of the Neuroi. At its mouth are settled those Hellenes who are called Tyritai.

Finally, the Neurians, to escape the influx of serpents, took refuge with their Scythian neighbors the Budinoi, and they have weird ways (Book IV):

> 105. The Neuroi practise the Scythian customs: and one generation before the expedition of Dareios it so befell them that they were forced to quit their land altogether by reason of serpents: for their land produced serpents in vast numbers, and they fell upon them in still larger numbers from the desert country above their borders; until at last being hard pressed they left their own land and settled among the Budinoi. These men it would seem are wizards; for it is said of them by the Scythians and by the Hellenes who are settled in the Scythian land that once in every year each of the Neuroi becomes a wolf for a few days and then returns again to his original form. For my part I do not believe them when they say this, but they say it nevertheless, and swear it moreover.

Oior's version seems to resolve all this by having the Neurians move into the Cimmerian lands about a generation before Darius came with his Persian army. He also pins the curse of the werewolf upon a battle in Scythia between the earth goddess and the moon goddess.

Chapter XI: In the Grip of the Neurian

11.01: (77–84) Latro is held, but Oior comes back swiftly to kill the attacker. Oior tells Latro to keep it secret. As Latro leaves he sees something horrible.

Back at the beach, a body has been discovered. The men rush to give it a burial. His name was Kekrops.

Looking back to the ridge, Latro sees a tall figure with a staff standing beside a shorter figure. The smaller one is the ghost of the dead bowman, Spu. Latro accuses him of killing the sailor Kekrops. The ghost denies it and calls Latro a Neurian.

The tall one tells Latro that his wife's mother sends her to speak with Latro, then leads the ghosts of bowman and sailor away.

The kybernates finds Latro and warns him a bowman named Spu plans to kill him.

Latro sees the goddess Europa, and another goddess who wears a helmet.

Latro writes all this beside the fire.

Onomasatics: Kekrops was an Athenian King of Greek mythology. He was said to be half man and half fish (or half snake). The founder of Athens, he was favored by Athena.

Herodotus writes that "spu" is Scythian for "eye" (Book IV, 27).

Myth: "A tall figure with a staff" seems to be Hades. His wife is Kore, the Maiden. His wife's mother is Demeter. A goddess who wears a helmet sounds like Athena.

Commentary: So many bodies, it seems like a murder mystery. Spu was plotting with another bowman. Was that bowman Oior? Oior's talk with Latro might have been the perfect set up for a killing. Spu's ghost claimed he did not kill Kekrops. Did Oior kill Kekrops, too? The *Mist* glossary says Kekrops is

"The sailor killed by the Neurian." Or was it someone else? Perhaps it was the snake-woman, who was so hungry for little Io.

So many gods. Hades is just doing his job, and Europa is near because of the ship bearing her name, but what does Athena have to do with this murder mystery?

Chapter XII: The Goddess of Love

12.01: (85–92) The ship *Europa* comes into the Bay of Peace at midmorning, planning a quick stop before travelling on to Tieup. The job is ferrying refugees back to Thought, including Kalleos and her twelve women. Hypereides tells Kalleos he bought Latro at Tower Hill after leaving Dolphins.

Kalleos is the model for the figure of Europa on the Bull depicted on the ship's sail.

There is a strange little social drama between Kalleos and Pindaros. When she suddenly starts treating him better, he puts the pieces together and guesses that his city of Hill has been spared annihilation by Thought.

Latro and the black man set up the toppled statue of the love goddess at another place, much later. Here is where Latro writes.

Onomastics: Kalleos means "my beauty" (*Mist* glossary).

Myth: The goddess of love is Aphrodite.

Geography: Tieup is the port of Thought (Athens).

Chapter XIII: Oh, Violet Crowned City!

13.01: (93–99) After Tieup, the smoking ruins of the city Thought. Pindaros mourns the destruction, even though his city had been an enemy. (The black man tells Latro they both helped in the destruction.)

Kalleos talks of having a deal to buy Latro. She tells of the oracle saying the Athenians would be safe behind walls of wood. She sets Latro to refurbishing her brothel (which is presumably where they restore the statue, as mentioned before). He meets Eurykles the Necromancer.

Geography: Thought is Athens.

Myth: Earth Shaker is Poseidon.

Pindaros: When the poet cries, "Oh, violet crowned!" (93), this echoes "receive ye violet-entwined crowns and drink-offerings of spring-gathered herbs" (Fragment of a Dithyramb, to be sung at Athens).

Chapter XIV: How Strange a Celebration

14.01: (100–106) The party starts. Latro is now Kalleos's slave. Kalleos tells Latro she was a slave herself, a child of the distant Budini. This relates to her red hair and blue eyes.

Little Io shows up. The black man gives her the wooden doll.

Latro writes at a broken chair near the courtyard door.

Budini: "Fair-haired barbarians inhabiting a densely forested tract northeast of the plains now held by the Sons of Scoloti" (*Mist* glossary).

Herodotus: The Budini, mentioned in passing in the previous quote relating to the Neuri, are now named directly. To Herodotus the Budini (Budinoi) are a forest-dwelling tribe in the area of Russia beyond the Tanaïs (the Don River). They are distinctive for their blue eyes and pale skin. From Book IV:

> 21. After one has crossed the river Tanaïs the country is no longer Scythia, but the first of the divisions belongs to the Sauromatai . . . Above these, holding the next division of land, dwell the Budinoi, who occupy a land wholly overgrown with forest consisting of all kinds of trees.

> 108. The Budinoi are a very great and numerous race, and are all very blue-eyed and fair of skin: and in their land is built a city of wood, the name of which is Gelonos, and each side of the wall is thirty furlongs in length and lofty at the same time, all being of wood; and the houses are of wood also and the temples; for there are in it temples of Hellenic gods furnished after Hellenic fashion with sacred images and altars and cells, all of wood; and they keep festivals every other year to Dionysos and celebrate the rites of Bacchus: for the Gelonians are originally Hellenes, and they removed from the trading stations on the coast and settled among the Budinoi; and they use partly the Scyth-

ian language and partly the Hellenic. The Budinoi however do not use the same language as the Gelonians, nor is their manner of living the same:

109, for the Budinoi are natives of the soil and a nomad people, and alone of the nations in these parts feed on fircones; but the Gelonians are tillers of the ground and feed on corn and have gardens, and resemble them not at all either in appearance or in complexion of skin. However by the Hellenes the Budinoi also are called Gelonians, not being rightly so called. Their land is all thickly overgrown with forests of all kinds of trees, and in the thickest forest there is a large and deep lake, and round it marshy ground and reeds.

This anthropological report shows the Hellenic Gelonians, with their frontier trade city Gelonos, and the semi-Hellenized Budini.

14.02: Later on, the partygoers play a game of throwing wine lees, the loser to tell a tale. Hypereides loses.
Commentary: Presumably Hypereides tells one of his war stories.

Chapter XV: The Woman Who Went Out

15.01: (107–113) Latro, awakened by the story-telling game, records the tale of prostitute Phye, about a wife who makes a clay doll to sleep with her husband while she prostitutes herself for money. When the clay doll becomes pregnant, the wife buries the doll under the apple tree. The husband inadvertently uses a similar spell to craft a substitute lover for his wife. Things go bad and both husband and wife are killed.
Satyricon: Storytelling at a party happens at least twice in this ancient Roman novel. At Trimalchio's dinner there is the tidbit about the Sibyl of Cumae (chapter 48), a story of a werewolf (chapter 62), and a story of witches (chapter 63); later, at a party on the ship, Eumolpus the poet tells the longer story of the widow grieving at the tomb of her husband and the soldier guarding crucified criminals (chapter 110–112). All these stor-

ies seem to have some bearing on Latro's tale.

Herodotus: The Babylonian maid in the story tells of the Babylonian marriage market, which the historian writes about in Book I:

> 199. Now the most shameful of the customs of the Babylonians is as follows: every woman of the country must sit down in the precincts of Aphrodite once in her life and have commerce with a man who is a stranger: and many women who do not deign to mingle with the rest, because they are made arrogant by wealth, drive to the temple with pairs of horses in covered carriages, and so take their place, and a large number of attendants follow after them; but the greater number do thus,—in the sacred enclosure of Aphrodite sit great numbers of women with a wreath of cord about their heads; some come and others go; and there are passages in straight lines going between the women in every direction, through which the strangers pass by and make their choice. Here when a woman takes her seat she does not depart again to her house until one of the strangers has thrown a silver coin into her lap and has had commerce with her outside the temple, and after throwing it he must say these words only: "I demand thee in the name of the goddess Mylitta": now Mylitta is the name given by the Assyrians to Aphrodite: and the silver coin may be of any value; whatever it is she will not refuse it, for that is not lawful for her, seeing that this coin is made sacred by the act: and she follows the man who has first thrown and does not reject any: and after that she departs to her house, having acquitted herself of her duty to the goddess, nor will you be able thenceforth to give any gift so great as to win her. So then as many as have attained to beauty and stature are speedily released, but those of them who are unshapely remain there much time, not being able to fulfil the law; for some of them remain even as much as three or four years: and in some parts of Cyprus too there is a custom similar to this.

Commentary: "The Woman Who Went Out" was published as a short story in *The Magazine of Fantasy & Science Fiction* (June

1985). It was the first glimpse of Latro's world.

15.02: (113–16) Eurykles the necromancer bets ten owls he can raise a ghost. The party prepares to visit a graveyard.

Chapter XVI: In the City

16.01: (117–24) Searching the graveyard, they come upon the exhumed corpse of a young woman. Eurykles will use his necromancy to solve the mystery. Phye leaves. The dead Thygater's eyes open, Latro touches her, and she stands.

Thygater says a wolf dug her up. A wolf named Man. Thygater says things that relate to the prophetic verses of the oracle of Dolphins, which Pindaros gives as:
"Wait not for horse and war,
But quit the land that bore you.
The eastern king shall rule your shore,
And yet give way before you." (122)

Eurykles and Thygater go toward the city. The others go away, with Latro and Pindaros returning to the brothel, where Io says Kalleos beat Phye terribly.

As dawn comes, Latro is writing.

Onomastics: Phye means "tall"; Thygater means "daughter" (*Mist* glossary).

Herodotus: As Kalleos mentioned the prophecy before, and Pindaros speaks on it here, the time has come for the historian's section on a Delphic prophecy to the Athenians about the coming war with Xerxes in Book VII (140-141):

> 140. For the Athenians had sent men to Delphi to inquire and were preparing to consult the Oracle; and after these had performed the usual rites in the sacred precincts, when they had entered the sanctuary and were sitting down there, the Pythian prophetess . . . uttered to them this oracle:
>
> "Why do ye sit, O ye wretched? Flee thou to the uttermost limits,
> Leaving thy home and the heights of the wheel-round city

behind thee!
Lo, there remaineth now nor the head nor the body in safety,—
Neither the feet below nor the hands nor the middle are left thee,—
All are destroyed together; for fire and the passionate War-god,
Urging the Syrian car to speed, doth hurl them to ruin.
Not thine alone, he shall cause many more great strongholds to perish,
Yes, many temples of gods to the ravening fire shall deliver,—
Temples which stand now surely with sweat of their terror down-streaming,
Quaking with dread; and lo! from the topmost roof to the pavement
Dark blood trickles, forecasting the dire unavoidable evil.
Forth with you, forth from the shrine, and steep your soul in the sorrow!"

141. Hearing this the men who had been sent by the Athenians to consult the Oracle were very greatly distressed; and as they were despairing by reason of the evil which had been prophesied to them, Timon the son of Androbulos, a man of the Delphians in reputation equal to the first, counselled them to take a suppliant's bough and to approach the second time and consult the Oracle as suppliants. The Athenians did as he advised and said: "Lord, we pray thee utter to us some better oracle about our native land, having respect to these suppliant boughs which we have come to thee bearing; otherwise surely we will not depart away from the sanctuary, but will remain here where we are now, even until we bring our lives to an end." When they spoke these words, the prophetess gave them a second oracle as follows:

"Pallas cannot prevail to appease great Zeus in Olympos,
Though she with words very many and wiles close-woven entreat him.
But I will tell thee this more, and will clench it with steel adamantine:
Then when all else shall be taken, whatever the boundary

of Kecrops
Holdeth within, and the dark ravines of divinest Kithairon,
A bulwark of wood at the last Zeus grants to the Trito-born goddess
Sole to remain unwasted, which thee and thy children shall profit.
Stay thou not there for the horsemen to come and the footmen unnumbered;
Stay thou not still for the host from the mainland to come, but retire thee,
Turning thy back to the foe, for yet thou shalt face him hereafter.
Salamis, thou the divine, thou shalt cause sons of women to perish,
Or when the grain is scattered or when it is gathered together."

The second oracle gives some hope ("bulwark of wood" and something about Salamis), and it seems that Wolfe's Pindaros nicely summarized both of the oracles in his short verse. The "bulwark of wood" was alluded to by Kalleos a few chapters earlier (chapter XIII, 97).

Mystery: Why did Kalleos beat Phye, and why so badly?

Commentary: Regarding the despoiled grave, it sounds like a Neurian wolfman is in the area.

Chapter XVII: On the Way to Advent

17.01: (125–34) Latro eats the first meal (at noon) at Kalleos's brothel. In conversation, he says no one should trust the gods: "[E]ven the best act in some twisted way. There's malice even in those who would be kind."

Hilaeira arrives, having walked from Tieup, with a letter from Hypereides to Kalleos.

Pindaros tells about the necromantic event of the night before. He thinks it was a setup. He explains that Phye knew Eurykles and told her story to lead in to Eurykles's bet; she was to further aid the fakery in one way or another.

Pindaros realizes Advent is where they must go.

Myth: "The Receiver of Many" is Hades.

Wolf: A badge of the Great Mother.

Geography: Advent is Eleusis, about 21 km/13 miles from Thought.

Mystery: Still not clear as to a motive for Kalleos to beat Phye.

Commentary: Latro's statement on the gods seems Socratic.

Chapter XVIII: Here in the Hall of the Great Mother

18.01: (135–43) At the temple, Hilaeira learns about being admitted to the mysteries, and that the next initial ceremony is in five days. After the sacrifice, the priest is shocked that the statue has moved its hand from resting on a stone boar to instead pointing at the floor. After this change, Latro senses that the air is "filled with soft yet heavy noises, as if some massive beast stirred and stamped where it could not be seen."

Latro is to sleep in the Royal House overnight.

Culture Note: The "archers" mentioned by the priest (137) are the barbarian mercenaries hired as Athenian police, mentioned in the Foreword (xiii).

Animal Emblems: The Great Mother has lions and wolves.

Herodotus: Here Wolfe seems to contradict Herodotus, who says the Persians had burned the temple at Eleusis in the weeks before the Battle of Clay (Book IX):

> 65. When the Persians were turned to flight at Plataia by the Lacedemonians, they fled in disorder to their own camp and to the palisade which they had made in the Theban territory: and it is a marvel to me that, whereas they fought by the side of the sacred grove of Demeter, not one of the Persians was found to have entered the enclosure or to have been slain within it, but round about the temple in the unconsecrated ground fell the greater number of the slain. I suppose (if one ought to suppose anything about divine things) that the goddess herself refused to receive them, because they had set fire to the temple, that is to say the "palace" at Eleusis.

This is a curious detail that is only visible to readers who are comparing the text with Herodotus, or with other histories that uniformly agree that the Persians burned the "palace" at Eleusis. Latro's narrative gives no hint of fire damage or recent repair.

18.02: (144) Latro tries to detect the presence of the goddess, but there is only the sense of age.

Chapter XIX: In the Presence of the Goddess

19.01: (145–51) Latro lifts the trapdoor indicated by the statue and descends beside the sacred fire to meet a goddess, the Maiden. She says Latro's sword was blessed by Asopus. She says to beware her half-sister Auge, who has stolen the south from the Great Mother. As she leaves, Latro sees Minos, and a man with a bull's head.

Wolf: Wolf-killer, wolf-flower, wolf's tooth. Wolf-killer being Apollo; wolf-flower being the lupine the Maiden gives Latro; the wolf's tooth that Latro bears, an enigma.

Herodotus: Latro's Swift God is named Asopus. When Latro sees him in the river (end of Chapter I), there are two girls with him, just as Herodotus notes: "Asopos is said to have had two daughters born to him, Thebe and Egina" (Book V, 80).

In addition, it turns out that the river Asopus has some relation to the Battle of Clay (Plataea), since it runs through the area and was the line that neither side would cross until the fateful day, as revealed in Book IX:

> 59. Thus having spoken he [Mardonius] led on the Persians at a run, after they had crossed the Asopos, on the track of the Hellenes, supposing that these were running away from him; and he directed his attack upon the Lacedemonians and Tegeans only, for the Athenians, whose march was towards the plain, he did not see by reason of the hills. Then the rest of the commanders of the Barbarian divisions, seeing that the Persians had started to pursue the Hellenes, forthwith all raised the signals for battle and began to pursue, each as fast as they could, not

arranged in any order or succession of post.

Myth: King Celeos (or "Celeus"), was ruler of Eleusis when Demeter came to the area in search for her daughter. He was kind to her, even though she was disguised, so she revealed herself to him, making him one of her first priests and initiating the Eleusinian Mysteries. (Celeus was killed by Erichthonius in a war with Athens.)

A megaron is "[t]he public room of a type of ancient palace" (*Mist* glossary).

Regarding the goddess Auge, a few details are in order. This obscure deity's name means "Sunbeam." She was a princess in Arcadia. She was raped by Heracles, or maybe she consented. She became pregnant with the hero Telephus. She was sealed in a wooden chest that was thrown into the sea.

When the Maiden refers to Auge as her half-sister, she presumably means on her father's side. The Maiden (or Persephone) is the daughter of Zeus and Demeter. Auge was the daughter of Aleus, the grandson of Arcas, who was the son of Zeus and Callisto.

But Wolfe, in the *Mist* glossary, says that Auge is the Bearland name of the Huntress. Ah! The relation is still on the father's side: Artemis is the daughter of Zeus and Leda.

End of Part II

Synopsis of Part II: From meeting Hypereides to meeting the Maiden (chapter VII to XIX)

A new owner in Hypereides. Travel on sea. Oior and the werewolf episode. Ruins of city Thought. A brothel party. A graveyard adventure, with signs of werewolf. Walk to Advent. Meet the Maiden.

Part III

Chapter XX: In My Room

20.01: (155–60) An unknown amount of time later, Latro writes. He is a regular slave at Kalleos's place. Hilaeira is going to Advent that night, so presumably it is five days after the previous chapter. The Rope-Makers are looking for Latro. After Latro finishes sweeping, he is visited by the goddess of doves. She talks of Myrrha. She and Latro are in a red flower blossom.

Kalleos propositions Latro, but she falls asleep, and he writes.

Latro Memories: Childhood (156).

Myth: The goddess of doves is Aphrodite. Myrrha's son, unnamed in the telling to Latro, was Adonis. The flower he became is anemone. The goddess tells Latro she put the baby in a chest, but the Maiden stole him and ultimately killed him.

Chapter XXI: Eutaktos

21.01: (161–67) Soldiers barge in. Kalleos claims she paid nine minas for Latro (equivalent to 900 drachmas or 90 owls). Learning about Latro's memory, they demand his book. Rope Makers, they make prisoners of Latro, Io, and Eurykles.

Latro writes all this camped by a spring. A woman with torches and hounds beckons to him.

Chapter XXII: The Woman at the Crossroads

22.01: (168–74) Latro meets Enodia, the Dark Mother, who says she is an enemy of the earth goddess. She tells Latro that once she had heard the God in the Tree and she sought him but found Latro instead.

Represented by images of three women standing back to back, she shows him again her form as the virgin Huntress. She gives him a tiny snake to feed to her follower and sends him to a farmhouse for a wine sack and a cup. In exorcising the farm, Latro says the three are Dark Mother, Huntress, and Moon.

Eurykles says it is the dark of the moon. Latro secretly feeds him the snake.

Latro sleeps then awakens before dawn and writes.

Myth: Enodia, "the one in the streets," was an ancient Greek goddess associated with Artemis, Hecate, or Persephone. For our purposes, it is Hecate, but it is nice to see the linkage to Artemis as well.

Chapter XXIII: In the Village

23.01: (175–81) They halt to buy food at Acharnae, fifty stades (5 miles) from Advent, which will be the next stop. The innkeeper tells them there was a strange incident there the night before. It was the trouble Latro was part of.

Basias tells about Pausanias and the Persian meal. Eurykles tells about Neurians, saying they live east of the Sons of Scoloti.

Latro gets into a friendly wrestling bout with his guard Basias. Heracles gives him tips, including when to let Basias win. (Latro writes in the courtyard of the inn.)

Geography: Acharnae had a sanctuary or altar of Heracles (William Smith, *Dictionary of Greek and Roman Geography*, 1854).

Myth: The innkeeper mentions Sabaktes and Mormo. Sabaktes is a malevolent spirit that pestered the potter by destroying his work; Mormo was a female spirit, a bugbear named to frighten children from misbehaving. The *Mist* glossary lists Mormo and Sabaktes as servants of the Dark Mother.

Herodotus: The historian writes of Pausanias and the Persian meal in Book IX:

> 82. It is said moreover that this was done which here follows, namely that . . . Pausanias . . . ordered the bakers and the cooks to prepare a meal as they were used to do for Mardonios. Then when they did this as they had been commanded, it is said that Pausanias . . . ordered his own servants to prepare a Laconian meal; and as, when the banquet was served, the difference between the two was great, Pausanias laughed and sent for the commanders of the Hellenes; and when these had come together, Pau-

sanias said, pointing to the preparation of the two meals severally: "Hellenes, for this reason I assembled you together, because I desired to show you the senselessness of this leader of the Medes, who having such fare as this, came to us who have such sorry fare as ye see here, in order to take it away from us." Thus it is said that Pausanias spoke to the commanders of the Hellenes.

Heracles: Heracles was a divine hero, the greatest of all Greek heroes, the son of Zeus and Alcmene. He had many adventures, but his Twelve Labors are an impressive set.

Chapter XXIV: Why Did You Lose?

24.01: (182–86) Basias tells about the Battle of Clay, and Latro has flashes of memory, which leads to him having a fit. He learns he had led a hundred; his comrade Marcus, probably his second in command, had died; and another man, Umeri, had disappeared.

Eurykles is a tall, ugly woman. She arranges to sacrifice to a Rope Maker god, Aesculapius, to heal Latro.

Io tells Latro Eurykles is a man.

Herodotus: When Latro recalls "spearmen and bowmen with bodies painted white and red" he seems to be describing the Great King's Ethiopians from Book VII:

> 69. The Ethiopians had skins of leopards and lions tied upon them, and bows made of a slip of palm-wood, which were of great length, not less than four cubits, and for them small arrows of reed with a sharpened stone at the head instead of iron, the same stone with which they engrave seals: in addition to this they had spears, and on them was the sharpened horn of a gazelle by way of a spear-head, and they had also clubs with knobs upon them. Of their body they used to smear over half with white, when they went into battle, and the other half with red.

This passage comes from a fascinating section that lists the 47 ethnic groups making up the soldiers in the Great King's army.

Onomastics: Marcus is a Latin name meaning "warlike." Umeri is a Latin word for "shoulders."

Myth: Aesculapius was first a hero and later a god of medicine in ancient Hellas. In Homer's *Iliad* he was a physician at the Trojan War.

24.02: (186–87) The slaves are building an altar. Eutaktos intends to go to Advent the next day. The innkeeper tries to detect Latro's homeland through a process of elimination.

Geography: The innkeeper opines on Latro's homeland by identifying what he is not. A Hellene is a person of mainland Greece; Persepolis is "the capital of the Empire" (glossary); Riverland is Egypt; Horseland is Thessaly (glossary); Tall Cap Country is Phrygia in Asia Minor (Scott Wowra); Archers' Country remains a mystery (perhaps Scythia, presumed origin for the foreign bowmen hired as police by Athens); and Caria is in southwest Asia Minor.

In order to try and puzzle out Latro's place of orgin, we return to the section in Book VII where Herodotus lists the 47 ethnic groups making up the soldiers in the Great King's army. Of all these, one group remains unnamed:

> 76.... [sic] and they had small shields of raw ox-hide, and each man carried two hunting-spears of Lykian workmanship. On their heads they wore helmets of bronze, and to the helmets the ears and horns of an ox were attached, in bronze, and upon them also there were crests; and the lower part of their legs was wrapped round with red-coloured strips of cloth. Among these men there is an Oracle of Ares.

This unique lack of a name for the group has caused all sorts of speculation across the millennia, and many commentators have gone on the record with one guess or another. I suspect this unnamed group is Latro's.

Wolf: Another curious detail about section 76 is in those "hunting spears of Lykian workmanship" (Macaulay translation), which are seen in other translations as "two half-finished *lukiourgides* spears. These are javelins of a type used to hunt wolves (*lukoi*), or else they were made in Lycia" (Athenaeus, *The Learned Banqueters, Volume V, Book XI,* 3rd century AD). Rawlinson's translation: "two spears such as are used in wolf-hunting." Godley's translation: "each man carried two wolf-hunter's spears."

Chapter XXV: I, Eurykles, Write

25.01: (188–94) Eurykles writes because Latro has been forbidden. Eurykles tells of his life, how at age eleven he poisoned a bully at the suggestion of the Triple Goddess. He tells of the graveyard adventure, then of the recent healing sacrifice. Io witnessed what was said in the morning. Latro saw Aesculapius, who said he was not a god, but had been sent by the murderess of his mother and could do nothing.

The Rope Maker Eutaktos is shocked by this language. Eurykles is, too.

Eurykles is writing on the road to Megara, past Eleusis.

A messenger comes for Eutaktos, then lingers. He is Pasicrates, also a servant of the Triple Goddess.

Myth: The "murderess of his mother" is the Huntress (Artemis). Aesculapius was a son of Apollo and a mortal woman named Coronis ("Homeric Hymn 16"). When she cheated on him (with a mortal), Artemis blasted her. Apollo rescued the unborn child and birthed it himself (in a pattern seen with Zeus birthing Dionysus).

Geography: Megara is on the Isthmus of Corinth, about 10 miles from Eleusis.

Onomastics: Pasicrates means "Dominates Everyone."

Commentary: Though a son of Apollo, Aesculapius is resentfully working at the order of Artemis, here at least.

Chapter XXVI: Pasicrates

26.01: (195–200) The messenger gives the scroll back to Latro. They then have a race to a nearby tree. While Pasicrates is the protégé of Pausanias, he finds the attention of Eurykles familiar yet strange, as he struggles to explain to Basias and Latro. When Latro asks him how it is different, he notes, "I was watching a scarlet wildflower nod in the breeze; it seemed charged with meaning" (197).

As the march continues, Eurykles says he is changing his name to Drakon.

Latro writes while waiting outside the regent Pausanias's tent.

Myth: There are at least two red flowers in Greek Mythology, anemone and poppy. Both involve humans and supernatural lovers; both involve the death of the humans. Since anemone has been referenced in the text by the goddess of doves, that is the most likely.

Chapter XXVII: Pausanias

27.01: (201–209) It turns out regent Pausanias had a dream about Latro. In it the goddess Kore showed him Latro at the party and told him Latro forgets every day, and behind Latro stood Nike.

Pausanias says Eurykles is a spy and demands to know who got the reports. After a blow to the head, Eurykles answers that it was Artabazus.

Pausanias outlines the politics of four: Rope wants peace; the Great King wants peace and union; Io's city might want to support Rope; Latro serves the Great King.

Military Terms: Lochagos is "The officer commanding a lochos. Roughly, a captain" (*Mist* glossary); ouragos is "The second in command of an enomotia. Roughly, a platoon sargeant" (*Mist* glossary), the rank of Basias who guarded Latro (202).

Myth: Nike is the personification of victory. She is often depicted as a miniature in the hand of Athena or Zeus.

History: Artabazus was the Persian general who survived the Battle of Clay (Plataea) and led a retreat north, the army Latro was with in the first few chapters. He was rewarded by being made satrap of Hellespontine Phrygia, first of a dynasty.

Herodotus: Many months before the Battle of Clay, Artabazus found the city Potidaia in revolt and besieged it. The historian writes that the general tried a plan of treachery (Book VIII):

> 128. Having taken this city Artabazos set himself to attack Potidaia with vigour, and as he was setting himself earnestly to this work, Timoxeinos the commander of the troops from Skione concerted with him to give up the town by treachery. Now in what manner he did this at the first, I for my part am not able to say, for this is not reported; at last however it happened as follows. Whenever either Timoxeinos wrote a paper wishing to send it to Artabazos, or Artabazos wishing to send one to Timoxeinos, they wound it round by the finger-notches of an arrow, and then, putting feathers over the paper, they shot it to a place agreed upon between them. It came however to be found out that Timoxeinos was attempting by treachery to give up Potidaia; for Artabazos, shooting an arrow at the place agreed upon, missed this spot and struck a man of Potidaia in the shoulder; and when he was struck, a crowd came about him, as is apt to happen when there is fighting, and they forthwith took the arrow and having discovered the paper carried it to the commanders. Now there was present an allied force of the other men of Pallene also. Then when the commanders had read the paper and discovered who was guilty of the treachery, they resolved not openly to convict Timoxeinos of treachery, for the sake of the city of Skione, lest the men of Skione should be esteemed traitors for all time to come.

The plan failed, and the siege lasted three months. Then Artabazus tried the strategy of attacking during an unusually low tide, which led to disaster.

Chapter XXVIII: Mycale

28.01: (210–17) The regent puts the Latro trio into the care of Pasicrates. Basias, having been poisoned by hitting Eurykles, suffers.

Healer Kichesippos examines Latro and tells them of the Battle at Mycale, where the Hellenes found the barbarian fleet on the beach and struck.

Drakaina says they will march two or three days to Rope, and then travel two or three days to Acheron, where Pausanias will consult the dead.

Mycale is the site of a recent naval battle that the Great King lost. Not clear when it happened, perhaps on the same day as the Battle of Clay. Io is concerned for the black man, who would likely have been there if the Battle of Mycale came on a later day.

Commentary: The doctor's scientific speculation that Latro's condition is caused by a "splinter of bone" or "small arrowhead" points toward a literal "wolf tooth" that has been mentioned a few times. This thread suggests that Latro was actually bitten by a phantom wolf of Demeter, in such a way that the tooth broke off and remains lodged in Latro's skull.

Herodotus: On Mycale and Clay (Plataea), in Book IX:

> 90. Now on the same day on which the defeat took place at Plataia, another took place also, as fortune would have it, at Mycale in Ionia. For when the Hellenes who had come in the ships with Leotychides the Lacedemonian, were lying at Delos, there came to them as envoys from Samos Lampon the son of Thrasycles and Athenagoras the son of Archestratides and Hegesistratos the son of Aristagoras, who had been sent by the people of Samos without the knowledge either of the Persians or of the despot Theomestor the son of Androdamas, whom the Persians had set up to be despot of Samos. When these had been introduced before the commanders, Hegesistratos spoke at great length using arguments of all kinds, and saying that so soon as the Ionians should see them they would at once revolt from the Persians, and that the Barbarians would not wait for their attack; and if after all they did so, then the Hellenes would take a prize such as they would never take again hereafter; and appealing to the gods worshipped in common he endeavoured to persuade them to rescue from slavery men who were Hellenes and to drive away the Barbarian: and this he said was easy for them to do, for the ships of the enemy sailed badly and were no match for them in fight. Moreover if the Hellenes sus-

pected that they were endeavouring to bring them on by fraud, they were ready to be taken as hostages in their ships.

Chapter XXIX: The Silent Country

29.01: (218–24) Looking back, little Io says they had camped outside Tower Hill one night, then in the hills of Bearland the next night.

Going through a village the next day, Latro gets into a fight with the blacksmith, who is killed by a slave of the Rope Makers. This slave is Cerdon, who had seen the black god (Silenus) with Latro. Cerdon invites him to the local shrine of the Great Mother, and schedules an evening time to go.

Drakaina seduces Latro, and he desires her, yet he is unable. She mocks him and says she will try again when the moon is up.

Satyricon: Another curious point of similarity with the renowned Roman roguery: wherein the hero's impotence begins at chapter 126 and lasts until chapter 140.

Herodotus: The episode with Drakaina hints that she might have been inspired by an episode of Heracles in Scythia, told in Book IV of *The Histories:*

> 8. . . . Heracles came to the land now called Scythia; and as a storm came upon him together with icy cold, he drew over him his lion's skin and went to sleep. Meanwhile the mares harnessed in his chariot disappeared by a miraculous chance, as they were feeding.
>
> 9. Then when Heracles woke he sought for them; and having gone over the whole land, at last he came to the region which is called Hylaia; and there he found in a cave a kind of twofold creature formed by the union of a maiden and a serpent, whose upper parts from the buttocks upwards were those of a woman, but her lower parts were those of a snake. Having seen her and marvelled at her, he asked her then whether she had seen any mares straying anywhere; and she said that she had them herself and would not give them up until he lay with her; and Heracles lay with her on condition of receiving them. She then tried to

put off the giving back of the mares, desiring to have Heracles with her as long as possible, while he on the other hand desired to get the mares and depart; and at last she gave them back and said: "These mares when they came hither I saved for thee, and thou didst give me reward for saving them; for I have by thee three sons. Tell me then, what must I do with these when they shall be grown to manhood, whether I shall settle them here, for over this land I have power alone, or send them away to thee?" She thus asked of him, and he, they say, replied: "When thou seest that the boys are grown to men, do this and thou shalt not fail of doing right:—whichsoever of them thou seest able to stretch this bow as I do now, and to be girded with this girdle, him cause to be the settler of this land; but whosoever of them fails in the deeds which I enjoin, send him forth out of the land: and if thou shalt do thus, thou wilt both have delight thyself and perform that which has been enjoined to thee."

10. Upon this he drew one of his bows (for up to that time Heracles, they say, was wont to carry two) and showed her the girdle, and then he delivered to her both the bow and the girdle, which had at the end of its clasp a golden cup; and having given them he departed. She then, when her sons had been born and had grown to be men, gave them names first, calling one of them Agathyrsos and the next Gelonos and the youngest Skythes; then bearing in mind the charge given to her, she did that which was enjoined. And two of her sons, Agathyrsos and Gelonos, not having proved themselves able to attain to the task set before them, departed from the land, being cast out by her who bore them; but Skythes the youngest of them performed the task and remained in the land: and from Skythes the son of Heracles were descended, they say, the succeeding kings of the Scythians (Skythians): and they say moreover that it is by reason of the cup that the Scythians still even to this day wear cups attached to their girdles: and this alone his mother contrived for Skythes. Such is the story told by the Hellenes who dwell about the Pontus.

The god-favored Heracles and an ambitious lamia breeding a line of Scythian kings seems very topical. Also note that the middle son, Gelonos, has the same name as the city of the Budini, as covered in notes for chapter 14.01.

Chapter XXX: The Great Mother

30.01: (225–30) Cerdon meets Latro by the campfire, tells him about the government of Rope by the five judges, who each year declare a secret war against the slaves of a specific area. He claims Pasicrates is a Silent One.

As they set out to the secret meeting, Cerdon is struck by a viper. Cerdon sends Latro alone, urging him to touch the goddess.

The river is the Eurotas. Latro follows the path. He sees a lion, and it sees him. Then a fire, where children are singing and dancing. Then the child sacrifice begins.

Latro sees the Great Mother, daubing her fingers in the blood.

Latro tries to leave and is beaten. Before they can kill him, Rope Makers pour in, led by Drakaina.

Spartan Terms: "Silent One" seems to designate a member of the Krypteia, a sort of secret police; "Equal" is a translation of "Spartiate" (citizen).

Chapter XXXI: Mother Ge's Words

31.01: (231–37) The Rope Makers tear down the altar. As they try to leave, they are pelted with stones. They are bottled up. Drakaina is attacked and she disappears. The slaves press their attack. Latro hears their goddess. The goddess Ge sees him, and she says her daughter has told her what she promised Latro. He touches her and all see her.

She asks for a castration sacrifice and a man obliges. Ge pledges to make Pausanias king. The slaves leave. At dawn, Latro walks back to camp. Cerdon had died.

Military Term: Enomotia, a unit of about thirty shieldmen.

Latro Memory: "I was a child once more, confronted by the crone from the cave on the hill" (234).

Myth: Kore as another name for the Maiden, Queen of the

Dead.

Chapter XXXII: Here in Rope

32.01: (238-44) Latro, Drakaina, and Io in the city Rope. They visit the temple of Orthia (the Huntress), where they meet Gorgo, priestess (and queen). Latro says the wooden statue is angry at Drakaina, and Drakaina goes pale.

Pasicrates shows them a well that "changes men to women." Latro looks down it and sees three men penned there. They are the ambassadors of the Great King, thrown down.

Drakaina now wears a crimson gown of silk that previously "belonged to a noble lady of Susa" (244).

Drakaina tells Latro that he had given her a slave who died. It seems like she means Eurykles.

Spartan Term: Neighbors, a social class, after the *perioeci*, "dwellers around."

Dream: Latro had a dream the night before (239) but he fails to write it.

Myth: Orthia, a name for Artemis, but the statue, "[t]he famous wooden figure from which this name is derived originally represented Gaea" (*Mist* glossary).

Mystery: Why is the Huntress angry at Drakaina? She seems to have been performing admirably. Perhaps because Drakaina failed at keeping Latro from touching the goddess Ge.

Herodotus: The historian wrote about that well in Sparta, and another place in Athens, in Book VII:

> 133. Thus ran the oath which was taken by the Hellenes: Xerxes however had not sent to Athens or to Sparta heralds to demand the gift of earth, and for this reason, namely because at the former time when Dareios had sent for this very purpose, the one people threw the men who made the demand into the pit and the others into a well, and bade them take from thence earth and water and bear them to the king. For this reason Xerxes did not send men to make this demand. And what evil thing came upon the Athenians for having done this to the heralds, I am not

able to say, except indeed that their land and city were laid waste; but I do not think that this happened for that cause:

In a possible echo to Drakaina's crimson gown, Herodotus also wrote about a garment belonging to a noble lady of Susa (Book IX):

> 108. At that time, while he [Xerxes] was in Sardis, he had a passionate desire, as it seems, for the wife of Masistes, who was also there: and as she could not be bent to his will by his messages to her, and he did not wish to employ force because he had regard for his brother Masistes and the same consideration withheld the woman also, for she well knew that force would not be used towards her, then Xerxes abstained from all else, and endeavoured to bring about the marriage of his own son Dareios with the daughter of this woman and of Masistes, supposing that if he should do so he would obtain her more easily. Then having made the betrothal and done all the customary rites, he went away to Susa; and when he had arrived there and had brought the woman into his own house for Dareios, then he ceased from attempting the wife of Masistes and changing his inclination he conceived a desire for the wife of Dareios, who was daughter of Masistes, and obtained her: now the name of this woman was Artaÿnte.
>
> 109. However as time went on, this became known in the following manner:—Amestris the wife of Xerxes had woven a mantle, large and of various work and a sight worthy to be seen, and this she gave to Xerxes. He then being greatly pleased put it on and went to Artaÿnte; and being greatly pleased with her too, he bade her ask what she would to be given to her in return for the favours which she had granted to him, for she should obtain, he said, whatsoever she asked: and she, since it was destined that she should perish miserably with her whole house, said to Xerxes upon this: "Wilt thou give me whatsoever I ask thee for?" and he, supposing that she would ask anything rather than that which she did, promised this and swore to it. Then when he had sworn, she boldly asked

for the mantle; and Xerxes tried every means of persuasion, not being willing to give it to her, and that for no other reason but only because he feared Amestris, lest by her, who even before this had some inkling of the truth, he should thus be discovered in the act; and he offered her cities and gold in any quantity, and an army which no one else should command except herself. Now this of an army is a thoroughly Persian gift. Since however he did not persuade her, he gave her the mantle; and she being overjoyed by the gift wore it and prided herself upon it.

110. And Amestris was informed that she had it; and having learnt that which was being done, she was not angry with the woman, but supposing that her mother was the cause and that she was bringing this about, she planned destruction for the wife of Masistes. She waited then until her husband Xerxes had a royal feast set before him:—this feast is served up once in the year on the day on which the king was born, and the name of this feast is in Persian *tycta*, which in the tongue of the Hellenes means "complete"; also on this occasion alone the king washes his head, and he makes gifts then to the Persians:—Amestris, I say, waited for this day and then asked of Xerxes that the wife of Masistes might be given to her. And he considered it a strange and untoward thing to deliver over to her his brother's wife, especially since she was innocent of this matter; for he understood why she was making the request.

111. At last however as she continued to entreat urgently and he was compelled by the rule, namely that it is impossible among them that he who makes request when a royal feast is laid before the king should fail to obtain it, at last very much against his will consented; and in delivering her up he bade Amestris do as she desired, and meanwhile he sent for his brother and said these words: "Masistes, thou art the son of Dareios and my brother, and moreover in addition to this thou art a man of worth. I say to thee, live no longer with this wife with whom thou now livest, but I give thee instead of her my daughter; with her live as thy wife, but the wife whom thou now hast, do not keep; for it does not seem good to me

that thou shouldest keep her." Masistes then, marvelling at that which was spoken, said these words: "Master, how unprofitable a speech is this which thou utterest to me, in that thou biddest me send away a wife by whom I have sons who are grown up to be young men, and daughters one of whom even thou thyself didst take as a wife for thy son, and who is herself, as it chances, very much to my mind,—that thou biddest me, I say, send away her and take to wife thy daughter! I, O king, think it a very great matter that I am judged worthy of thy daughter, but nevertheless I will do neither of these things: and do not thou urge me by force to do such a thing as this: but for thy daughter another husband will be found not in any wise inferior to me, and let me, I pray thee, live still with my own wife." He returned answer in some such words as these; and Xerxes being stirred with anger said as follows: "This then, Masistes, is thy case,—I will not give thee my daughter for thy wife, nor yet shalt thou live any longer with that one, in order that thou mayest learn to accept that which is offered thee." He then when he heard this went out, having first said these words: "Master, thou hast not surely brought ruin upon me?"

112. During this interval of time, while Xerxes was conversing with his brother, Amestris had sent the spearmen of Xerxes to bring the wife of Masistes, and she was doing to her shameful outrage; for she cut away her breasts and threw them to dogs, and she cut off her nose and ears and lips and tongue, and sent her back home thus outraged.

113. Then Masistes, not yet having heard any of these things, but supposing that some evil had fallen upon him, came running to his house; and seeing his wife thus mutilated, forthwith upon this he took counsel with his sons and set forth to go to Bactria together with his sons and doubtless some others also, meaning to make the province of Bactria revolt and to do the greatest possible injury to the king: and this in fact would have come to pass, as I imagine, if he had got up to the land of the Bactrians and Sacans before he was overtaken, for they were much attached to him, and also he was the governor of the Bactrians: but Xerxes being informed that he was doing this,

sent after him an army as he was on his way, and slew both him and his sons and his army. So far of that which happened about the passion of Xerxes and the death of Masistes.

End of Part III

Synopsis of Part III: From Kalleos to Rope (chapter XX to XXXII)

A new owner in Kalleos. Visit by dove goddess. Taken by soldiers. Meet Triple Goddess. Tips from Heracles. Memories of the Battle at Clay. Seeing Aesculapius. Touching Ge so the slaves of the Rope Makers can see her. Visit Rope.

Part IV

Chapter XXIII: Through This Shadowed Gorge

33.01: (247–48) After an unknown gap of time, and at a place very far away from Rope, they are on the river Acheron, preparing to make sacrifice. Latro writes of a dream of being on a ship, opening a hatch and going down to a cavern where a queen and king are enthroned. Little Io says the ship is like the one they took.

Geography: The Acheron is in the Epirus region of northwest Greece, west of Thessaly.

33.02: (248–53) At the animal sacrifice, an armored king comes out of the rock. Drakaina falls into a fit and speaks a prophetic answer:

"Nephew, seek peace and not death.
Nor drink from the blue cup of Lethe.
Ask who will make the fortress yield,
To those that fought at Fennel Field."

When the shade of King Cleomenes returns to the rock, he has an attendant who looks familiar to Latro.

Pasicrates gives his interpretation of the prophecy, that Rope should send a token force to aid the siege of Sestos. Soon there is a camp announcement that Pasicrates will lead a hundred volunteers to aid the siege of Sestos across the water. Latro, Io, and Drakaina will go.

In talking with little Io, Latro realizes that the ghost he saw following King Cleomenes was Eurykles.

Io refers to having seen Kekrops "after the sea monster killed him." She gives her interpretation of the utterance: Cleomenes wants real peace, not sending men.

Drakaina gives her interpretation: Real peace will come through an alliance between Rope and the Empire; that the key to peace is Demaratus, the true heir to the younger crown of Rope, who is also one of Xerxes's advisors. If Demaratus were made the younger king, peace would result. If it had happened two years earlier, "the whole war might have been prevented."

History: Cleomenes was a King of Sparta (c. 519 BC–c. 490 BC). After his death, he was succeeded by his half-brother Leonidas, who then married Cleomenes's daughter Gorgo.

Herodotus: In Book VI, the historian writes on the terrible death of Cleomenes:

> 75. The Lacedemonians, hearing that Cleomenes was acting thus, were afraid, and proceeded to bring him back to Sparta to rule on the same terms as before: but when he had come back, forthwith a disease of madness seized him (who had been even before this somewhat insane), and whenever he met any of the Spartans, he dashed his staff against the man's face. And as he continued to do this and had gone quite out of his senses, his kinsmen bound him in stocks. Then being so bound, and seeing his warder left alone by the rest, he asked him for a knife; and the warder not being at first willing to give it, he threatened him with that which he would do to him afterwards if he did not; until at last the warder fearing the threats, for he was one of the Helots, gave him a knife. Then Cleomenes, when he had received the steel, began to maltreat himself from the legs upwards: for he went on cutting his flesh lengthways from the legs to the thighs and from the thighs to the loins and flanks, until at last he came to the belly; and cutting this into strips he died in that manner. And this happened, as most of the Hellenes report, because he persuaded the Pythian prophetess to advise that which was done about Demaratos; but as the Athenians alone report, it was because when he invaded Eleusis he laid waste the sacred enclosure of the goddesses; and according to the report of the Argives, because from their sanctuary dedicated to Argos he caused to come down those of the Argives who had fled for refuge from the battle and slew them, and also set fire to the grove itself, holding it in no regard.

The king went mad and killed himself with a knife. In the Athenian version, the insanity was because when the king had invaded Eleusis, he had destroyed the sacred enclosure of the goddesses, which sounds similar to what the Persians did later.

Possession: The detail of Eurykles's soul going to Hades when Eurykles is not yet dead seems like a case of possession. This is like a bit in Dante's *Inferno,* where the soul of a living man is suffering in Hell while a demon possesses his body up on Earth.

> He answered: 'I am Friar Alberic—
>   He of the fruit grown in the orchard fell—
>   And here am I repaid with date for fig.'
> 'Ah!' said I to him, 'art thou dead as well?'
>   'How now my body fares,' he answered me,
>   'Up in the world, I have no skill to tell;
> For Ptolomæa has this quality—
>   The soul oft plunges hither to its place
>   Ere it has been by Atropos set free.
> And that more willingly from off my face
>   Thou mayst remove the glassy tears, know, soon
>   As ever any soul of man betrays
> As I betrayed, the body once his own
>   A demon takes and governs until all
>   The span allotted for his life be run.
> Into this tank headlong the soul doth fall;
>   And on the earth his body yet may show
>   Whose shade behind me wintry frosts enthral.
>   (*Inferno,* Canto XXIII, lines 118–35)

Mystery: Little Io reveals that Kekrops is thought to have been killed by a sea monster, which is curious because the text has not shown any sea monsters.

33.03: (253) Latro is called to a meeting. Io tells Latro some camp gossip that the regent's sorcerer has come by ship.

Chapter XXXIV: In the Regent's Tent

34.01: (254–62) Latro meets Tisamenus of Elis, the Hellenic mantis to the regent. The three men have a symposium, first talking about the griffin carving that leads to a discussion about the monster's origin in a land of the Sons of Scoloti, north and west of the Issedonians. Tisamenus says Latro remembers the monster, somehow.

Pausanias, trying to figure out his connection to Latro, wonders if they were born on the same day. He says he is twenty-eight, and Latro admits he thinks himself younger than that.

Delving deeper, Latro ends up describing the duality system of Ahura Mazda (the good god) and Angra Manyu (the evil god), but then he states that logically, if Ahura Mazda exists, then all things serve him.

Pausanias and his mantis press Latro on his influence with the gods. Latro responds with a metaphor, wherein there is a great palace, and a beggar boy, he himself, squats outside of it. Latro says that Ahura Mazda is not the king of the palace: "The servants are the lords of the palace. Once a cook gave me meat, and a scullion, bread. I've even seen the steward, Highness, with my own eyes." Pausanias takes this steward to be himself, and is impressed.

Captain Nepos arrives, to arrange passage on his ship, the *Nausicaa*.

Later Tisamenus whispers to Latro, "Kill the man with the wooden foot!"

Herodotus: The surprising luxury within Pausanias's tent evokes another scene from the aftermath of the Battle of Clay (Plataea) in Book IX:

> 80. Pausanias made a proclamation that none should lay hands upon the spoil, and he ordered the Helots to collect the things together. They accordingly dispersed themselves about the camp and found tents furnished with gold and silver, and beds overlaid with gold and overlaid with silver, and mixing-bowls of gold, and cups and other drinking vessels....
>
> 81. ... Pausanias however had ten of each thing set apart and given to him, that is women, horses, talents, camels, and so also of the other things.
>
> 82. It is said moreover that this was done which here follows, namely that Xerxes in his flight from Hellas had left to Mardonios the furniture of his own tent.

The contrast of a Spartan tent containing Oriental opulence is here explained by the historian telling that Pausanias had recently won war trophies, including items from Xerxes, after the same battle where Latro got his mysterious head wound.

When the talk turns to the griffins, the Issedonians, and the Sons of Scoloti (Scythians), these details are mentioned in Book IV:

> 13. Aristeas... said in the verses which he composed, that he came to the land of the Issedonians being possessed by Phoebus, and that beyond the Issedonians dwelt Arimaspians, a one-eyed race, and beyond these the gold-guarding griffins, and beyond them the Hyperboreans extending as far as the sea: and all these except the Hyperboreans, beginning with the Arimaspians, were continually making war on their neighbours, and the Issedonians were gradually driven out of their country by the Arimaspians and the Scythians by the Issedonians, and so the Kimmerians, who dwelt on the Southern Sea, being pressed by the Scythians left their land. Thus neither does he agree in regard to this land with the report of the Scythians.

This matches what was said to Latro in the tent, with the addition of naming the Arimaspians. It seems unlikely that Latro visited this distant place, yet he recognizes some of it, presumably because he had seen and discussed the griffin statuette in the tent of Xerxes. Herodotus also has something to say about the Issedonians:

> 26. The Issedonians are said to have these customs:— when a man's father is dead, all the relations bring cattle to the house, and then having slain them and cut up the flesh, they cut up also the dead body of the father of their entertainer, and mixing all the flesh together they set forth a banquet. His skull however they strip of the flesh and clean it out and then gild it over, and after that they deal with it as a sacred thing and perform for the dead man great sacrifices every year. This each son does for his father, just as the Hellenes keep the day of memorial for the dead. In other respects however this race also is said to

live righteously, and their women have equal rights with the men.

27. These then also are known; but as to the region beyond them, it is the Issedonians who report that there are there one-eyed men and gold-guarding griffins; and the Scythians report this having received it from them, and from the Scythians we, that is the rest of mankind, have got our belief; and we call them in Scythian language Arimaspians, for the Scythians call the number one *arima* and the eye *spu*.

Timestamp: Latro is younger than twenty-eight, perhaps twenty to twenty-five.

Myth: Latro seems remarkably well versed on the Persian religion of Ahura Mazda. Presumably this was something he picked up while in the army of the Great King. Yet he is also extending it into a monotheism.

Dunsany: Latro's brief lines on the metaphorical palace requires unpacking (If the "steward" is Pausanias, then who are the "cook" and the "scullion" who aided Latro? Perhaps just the most recent givers of meat and bread.). Setting that aside, the trope itself echoes "The Exiles Club" (1916) by Lord Dunsany, wherein the narrator in modern London is invited to visit an exclusive club of exiled kings, only to learn through embarrassing mistakes that the exiled kings are mere servants to the exiled gods of the upper floors.

Onomastics: Nepos is Greek for "nephew" (it led to the term "nepotism").

Odysseus: The *Nausicaa* is named after a princess featured in *The Odyssey,* which is romantic for that association, but her name means "burner of ships."

Chapter XXXV Ships Can Sail Dry Land

35.01: (263–69) The *Nausicaa* is crossing the isthmus this day, after waiting all of the day before. Io reveals that she and Latro have been at this city before, brought there by the soldiers who had taken them away from the Rope Makers' slaves. This is

Tower Hill where Hypereides took possession of them.

Latro, little Io, and Drakaina see the sights.

Drakaina meets the lochagos Hippagretas, then sells information to Corustas (that the regent and his hundred men are heading to Sestos; and the gist of the dream) for eight owls.

Geography: Tower Hill is Corinth. It had a temple of Apollo, but it was most famous for its temple of Aphrodite.

Myth: Corustas mentions gods the Warrior and the Sun (268). The Warrior sounds like the god of war, Ares; the Sun is probably Apollo, given the temple, but it might be Helios.

Onomastics: Hippagretas is a name that was originally a rank for a leader of 100 horsemen.

Commentary: Drakaina seems like a double agent here, since Corinth was part of the alliance against the Empire. Then again, the main mission is to disrupt the work Pausanias does for the earth goddess.

Chapter XXXVI: To Reach the Hot Gates

36.01: (270–77) On the ship, Latro has another chance to wrestle. Pasicrates tosses him overboard. Underwater he meets Thoe, daughter of Nereus. By the time he escapes her, the ship is gone. He swims, north, lands on a beach. Latro completes his bout and wins two out of three falls, earning the right to perform the sacrifice.

Geography: The Crimson Men are Phoenicians, mainly in the area that would later become Lebanon, but also Carthage.

Myth: Drakaina had said the world was shaped by Phanes (275). Phanes is part of the Orphic tradition, and far removed from the creation myths written by Homer and Hesiod. Phanes has an animal totem of the serpent. Phanes is also hermaphroditic. These details alone explain much.

Thoe, meaning "quick, nimble," was one of the daughters of the Oceanid Doris and the sea-god Nereus; Nereus was an early sea god, replaced by Poseidon.

Heracles: As "The Old Man of the Sea," Nereus links to the labors of Heracles. The hero has to wrestle with him.

Chapter XXXVII Leonidas, Lion of Rope

37.01: (277–83) Latro makes the prayer to Leonidas, then all eat. He learns Leonidas was a hero, killed at this location called Hot Gates, a sulfurous hot spring. Latro sees ghosts combing their hair and exercising. Pasicrates says this is where the 300 Rope Makers fell, along with a few thousand helot slaves who had been armed against all convention. Latro weeps at hearing about it, and says he must have been there, on the side of the Great King.

The mantis appears to Latro. Latro has a vision of being at the battle, where he has two javelins, a helmet, back and breast plates, and a rectangular shield. He shouts to his hundred about how the Immortals are away. As battle begins, he cries out the name "Cassius!" It seems that Latro fights King Leonidas himself.

Awakening later, he writes down his episode, from the wrestling on the ship, through the meeting with Thoe the Nereid, to this dream/memory of the battle.

Geography: Hot Gates is Thermopylae.

History: Latro's shout of "Cassius" is complicated. At first glance, he might be referring to a personal friend at the battle, or one who had died previously, but the utterance seems more like a group command or a personal war cry.

Cassius was the name of a family that influenced the Roman Republic from the beginning to the end, the first one being Spurius Cassius Viscellinus. One of the most distinguished men of the early republic, this Cassius was consul three times, celebrated two triumphs, and crafted the first agrarian law; however, he was convicted of reaching for regal power and executed in 485 BC, just six years before the Battle of Plataea. He left behind three sons, who seem to have become plebeians.

Herodotus: The historian describes how scouts saw the Spartans at Thermopylae combing their hair and exercising (Book VII):

207. These, I say, had intended to do thus: and meanwhile the Hellenes at Thermopylai, when the Persian had come near to the pass, were in dread, and deliberated about making retreat from their position. To the rest of the Peloponnesians then it seemed best that they should go to the Peloponnese and hold the Isthmus in guard; but Leonidas, when the Phokians and Locrians were indignant at this opinion, gave his vote for remaining there, and for sending at the same time messengers to the several States bidding them to come up to help them, since they were but few to repel the army of the Medes.

208. As they were thus deliberating, Xerxes sent a scout on horseback to see how many they were in number and what they were doing; for he had heard while he was yet in Thessaly that there had been assembled in this place a small force, and that the leaders of it were Lacedemonians together with Leonidas, who was of the race of Heracles. And when the horseman had ridden up towards their camp, he looked upon them and had a view not indeed of the whole of their army, for of those which were posted within the wall, which they had repaired and were keeping a guard, it was not possible to have a view, but he observed those who were outside, whose station was in front of the wall; and it chanced at that time that the Lacedemonians were they who were posted outside. So then he saw some of the men practising athletic exercises and some combing their long hair: and as he looked upon these things he marvelled, and at the same time he observed their number: and when he had observed all exactly, he rode back unmolested, for no one attempted to pursue him and he found himself treated with much indifference. And when he returned he reported to Xerxes all that which he had seen.

209. Hearing this Xerxes was not able to conjecture the truth about the matter, namely that they were preparing themselves to die and to deal death to the enemy so far as they might; but it seemed to him that they were acting in a manner merely ridiculous; and therefore he sent for Demaratos the son of Ariston, who was in his camp, and

when he came, Xerxes asked him of these things severally, desiring to discover what this was which the Lacedemonians were doing: and he said: "Thou didst hear from my mouth at a former time, when we were setting forth to go against Hellas, the things concerning these men; and having heard them thou madest me an object of laughter, because I told thee of these things which I perceived would come to pass; for to me it is the greatest of all ends to speak the truth continually before thee, O king. Hear then now also: these men have come to fight with us for the passage, and this is it that they are preparing to do; for they have a custom which is as follows;—whenever they are about to put their lives in peril, then they attend to the arrangement of their hair. Be assured however, that if thou shalt subdue these and the rest of them which remain behind in Sparta, there is no other race of men which will await thy onset, O king, or will raise hands against thee: for now thou art about to fight against the noblest kingdom and city of those which are among the Hellenes, and the best men." To Xerxes that which was said seemed to be utterly incredible, and he asked again a second time in what manner being so few they would fight with his host. He said; "O king, deal with me as with a liar, if thou find not that these things come to pass as I say."

After this preview, the historian describes the fight that stretched on for days; how the Persians found a path to sneak up behind the Greeks with a force (Wolfe gives this job to the Immortals); and how the Greeks reacted to this with a final charge:

223. Xerxes meanwhile, having made libations at sunrise, stayed for some time, until about the hour when the market fills, and then made an advance upon them; for thus it had been enjoined by Epialtes, seeing that the descent of the mountain is shorter and the space to be passed over much less than the going round and the ascent. The Barbarians accordingly with Xerxes were advancing to the attack; and the Hellenes with Leonidas, feeling that they were going forth to death, now advanced out much further than at first into the broader part of the defile; for when the fence of the wall was being guarded, they on

the former days fought retiring before the enemy into the narrow part of the pass; but now they engaged with them outside the narrows, and very many of the Barbarians fell: for behind them the leaders of the divisions with scourges in their hands were striking each man, ever urging them on to the front. Many of them then were driven into the sea and perished, and many more still were trodden down while yet alive by one another, and there was no reckoning of the number that perished: for knowing the death which was about to come upon them by reason of those who were going round the mountain, they displayed upon the Barbarians all the strength which they had, to its greatest extent, disregarding danger and acting as if possessed by a spirit of recklessness.

224. Now by this time the spears of the greater number of them were broken, so it chanced, in this combat, and they were slaying the Persians with their swords; and in this fighting fell Leonidas, having proved himself a very good man, and others also of the Spartans with him, men of note, of whose names I was informed as of men who had proved themselves worthy, and indeed I was told also the names of all the three hundred.

Chapter XXXVIII Wet Weather to Sestos

38.01: (284–90) They sail by a volcanic isle called "Boat." After getting through a storm, the captain tells Latro about Polycrates, who had sacrificed his emerald ring to the sea, only to have it rejected. The captain tries to buy Latro from Pasicrates for six minas, but the offer is refused. At nightfall they land at the beach near Sestos.

Little Io mentions her doll, which is broken.

Latro remembers his family's god was Lar. He remembers lying under the wolfskin.

Timestamp: No moon and no stars, only this drizzle.

Geography: The volcanic island called "Boat" is not on the map supplied in the book. It seems like it must be either Santorini or Milos. Santorini is the one that blew up and ruined Minoan Civilization, and in overhead outline it looks something like a crescent boat. Milos is the one on which was later found the famous statue of Venus.

Herodotus: The historian tells the story of Polycrates and the rejected sacrifice Book III, 39–43; 120–126.

Wolf: Latro's home has a wolfskin.

Chapter XXXIX Engines of War

39.01: (291–99) The next morning, Latro goes with Pasicrates and Drakaina to meet Xanthippos, the strategist from Thought. Then Latro's group, plus Io, examine the walls of Sestos. Io admits she already knows the way in.

Drakaina tells the story of the Golden Ram.

Latro learns that Hypereides is among the siege engineers; he meets the chief builder, Ialtos; and Io spots the black man.

Chapter XL: Among Forgotten Friends

40.01: (300–306) Latro meets the black man. Drakaina discovers the man speaks Aram, and that he learned it in three years of army life. Asked how he met Latro, he says he saw that a god had touched him.

Pasicrates wants the black man to go into the besieged city; the black man refuses unless Latro and Io go with him. Deadlocked, they look at a siege engine the black man is building, a tower on wheels. Oior the bowman is also there.

Later, Pasicrates demands Latro hand over his sword. Latro refuses. Force is used. Latro escapes the tent and runs to the hills, where he writes while waiting for moonrise.

Commentary: Pasicrates has been working against Latro, earlier throwing him overboard, now trying to disarm him. He is clearly an agent of his goddess the Huntress (as first noted in chapter XXV), working against the earth goddess.

Chapter XLI: We Are in Sestos

41.01: (307–12) Latro awakes from a dream of love, a dream that might be a missing memory of the night he wore a satyr mask (in chapter IV). He thinks of Jove the god. He finds he had been sleeping next to a bottomless pit.

Then he encounters the Maiden. She returns his scroll. She says the gods are meddling now because "the Unseen God wanes, and we are no longer lost in his light" (309). She demands a wolf sacrifice. She tells him how it will happen. He agrees.

He runs around the city wall until he sees a woman and child. A man with a recently cut-off hand tries to stop him. Latro hands his sword to the child. Then he, Io, and the woman are drawn through the wall.

Here he writes.

Myth: Jove is the Roman name for Zeus.

Wolf: Far off, a wolf howled (307).

Chapter XLII: Though Not Without Aid

42.01: (313–21) Latro must face three warriors in bare-handed combat. He says a prayer to the Maiden and sees two ghosts come to help him. One is Odysseus, who says, "We need more blood, for Peleus's son." This implies that the other ghost is Achilles.

Latro wins. Artaÿctes invites him to join in the escape to Susa. Latro agrees.

Oschos offers to show him around.

Io plans to stay behind.

Myth: "Peleus's son" is Achilles. Achilles was killed by Trojan prince Paris near the end of the Trojan War. But Achilles, a Myrmidon, had an intra-Hellenic feud with Agamemnon, leader of the Achaeans.

Odysseus: His ghost shows up to aid Latro.

Herodotus: When Drakaina says "the people are boiling the straps from the beds," she echoes the historian describing the siege of Sestos (Book IX):

> 117. When however autumn came and the siege still went on, the Athenians began to be vexed at being absent from their own land and at the same time not able to conquer the fortress, and they requested their commanders to lead them away home; but these said that they would not do

so, until either they had taken the town or the public authority of the Athenians sent for them home: and so they endured their present state.

118. Those however who were within the walls had now come to the greatest misery, so that they boiled down the girths of their beds and used them for food.

Latro's narrative gives a detail about Artaÿctes sacrilegiously using tombs to house his concubines that is something like an episode in Book IX, but different enough to warrant comment. Herodotus describes how the Persian governor desecrated the temple at Elaeus, a place that is many miles down the coast from Sestos. The Elaeus temple was for Protesilaos, the first Hellene to set foot on land during the Trojan War.

116. And of the province Artaÿctes was despot, as governor under Xerxes, a Persian, but a man of desperate and reckless character, who also had practised deception upon the king on his march against Athens, in taking away from Elaius the things belonging to Protesilaos the son of Iphiclos. For at Elaius in the Chersonese there is the tomb of Protesilaos with a sacred enclosure about it, where there were many treasures, with gold and silver cups and bronze and raiment and other offerings, which things Artaÿctes carried off as plunder, the king having granted them to him. And he deceived Xerxes by saying to him some such words as these: "Master, there is here the house of a man, a Hellene, who made an expedition against thy land and met with his deserts and was slain: this man's house I ask thee to give to me, that every one may learn not to make expeditions against thy land." By saying this it was likely that he would easily enough persuade Xerxes to give him a man's house, not suspecting what was in his mind: and when he said that Protesilaos had made expedition against the land of the king, it must be understood that the Persians consider all Asia to be theirs and to belong to their reigning king. So when the things had been given him, he brought them from Elaius to Sestos, and he sowed the sacred enclosure for crops and occupied it as his own; and he himself, whenever he came to Elaius, had

commerce with women in the inner cell of the temple. And now he was being besieged by the Athenians, when he had not made any preparation for a siege nor had been expecting that the Hellenes would come; for they fell upon him, as one may say, inevitably.

The connection to the Trojan War might explain why the ghosts of Odysseus and Achilles, both heroes of the Trojan War, are showing up to help Latro. In addition to answering Latro's prayer to the Maiden, of course.

Herodotus says directly that Sestos was the anchor point for the pontoon bridge across the Hellespont, but he seems vague as to whether the Persian headquarters had been moved to Elaeus, so it is not clear whether the siege is of Sestos or Elaeus.

Chapter XLIII: A Soldier of the Mist

43.01: (322-26) Latro and the woman in purple go out to join a group of horsemen. Latro hears a man translating a rousing speech about Ahura Mazda, using Latro's native language. He speaks of "Ash," a god, perhaps.

Once outside the gate, Latro sees on his side a few dozen footsoldiers with oblong shields, led by one who bears an eagle on a staff. But then they all realize they are a decoy, and Artaÿctes has sacrificed them.

The werewolf with a broken back is tearing at the woman in purple. The monster asks Latro to kill him, and Latro sees the Maiden so he does so. But the woman in purple is dying. A thick snake comes out of her mouth. The woman says she is Eurykles and dies.

A voice says "Lucius." Latro finds a dying man beside the broken eagle standard, a man who wears a lion skin, speaks his own language, and calls him Lucius.

Myth: The translated speech of Artaÿctes warns the warriors against cowardice, "Surely Ash will know of it!" (323). Since the speaker is talking about Ahura Mazda, this "Ash" is in Zoroastrianism.

It is probably a typo for "Asha," which is a sort of archangel of Truth and Righteousness, one of a group of seven beings in later centuries called "amschaspands."

Animal Emblems: The case of wolf-man and snake-woman first seems ambiguous. Wolf is an emblem of Demeter, and snake is an emblem of Hecate, and in their last encounter the two are harming each other. On the other hand, both are transformed, which smacks of Hecate. (Traditionally werewolves are moon sensitive, which seems appropriate here.) If both wolf-man and snake-woman are moon agents, it would make a certain kind of sense that the Maiden would want the wolf-man to be killed (as a point against fake wolves, perhaps).

With regard to the sacrifice, note how earlier, for the animal sacrifice, a trick was used to make the animal agree to the sacrifice by nodding its head (Chapter XVIII, 140). Here the wolf-man begs for the sacrifice, calling on previous promises.

Commentary: The name "Lucius" suggests that Latro and the dying man are both Romans. The eagle standard suggests a Roman Legion. That the man wore a lion's skin implies he was an aquilifer, the standard bearer.

Filling in the gaps, it appears that Latro's military unit retreated after the Battle of Clay (Plataea), but the few dozen did not go with Artabazos as Latro did. They must have independently taken a ship to Sestos.

End of Part IV

Synopsis of Part IV: From Acheron to Sestos (chapter XXXIII to XLII)

Sacrifice at river Acheron. Meet Tisamenus of Elis, mantis to the regent. Ships crossing the isthmus. Meeting Thoe, daughter of Nereus. Visions at the Hot Gates. Sestos. Betrayal by Artaÿctes. Meeting lost friends.

APPENDICES TO SOLDIER OF THE MIST

Appendix L1-1: Preliminary Notes

As should be clear throughout this study, Herodotus, who is honored at the beginning of *Soldier of the Mist* with both a dedication and an epigraph, wrote the history that produced a large impact on the novel in ways too many to count. Despite this, there is a notable contradiction as to the condition of the Temple of Demeter at Eleusis after the Battle of Plataea (Book IX):

> 65. When the Persians were turned to flight at Plataia by the Lacedemonians, they fled in disorder to their own camp and to the palisade which they had made in the Theban territory: and it is a marvel to me that, whereas they fought by the side of the sacred grove of Demeter, not one of the Persians was found to have entered the enclosure or to have been slain within it, but round about the temple in the unconsecrated ground fell the greater number of the slain. I suppose (if one ought to suppose anything about divine things) that the goddess herself refused to receive them, because they had set fire to the temple, that is to say the "palace" [anaktoron] at Eleusis.

The historian states that the Persians had burned the temple at Eleusis before the Battle of Plataea; yet Wolfe's novel shows no sign of the temple having suffered such a calamity in chapter XVIII The Hall of the Great Mother.

Other historians agree with Herodotus, but pinning down

the destruction seems tricky. It seems that the Telesterion, the great hall of the temple, was destroyed by the Persians in 480 BC. It was rebuilt by Pericles some time later. Other structures are the Temple of Kore (hewn from rock) and the Plutonion, a sacred cave with a chamber beneath it.

Another contention between Wolfe and Herodotus comes with the siege of Sestos at the end of the novel, wherein Wolfe resolves ambiguities in Herodotus by placing the siege at Sestos rather than at the implied Elaeus.

These cases are on the surface.

In contrast, Wolfe shows a subtle playing of themes in Herodotus. In the opening paragraphs of his histories, Herodotus attempts to trace the beginning of the conflict between Hellenes and Barbarians, and he finds it in a series of four rape/abductions: that of Io by the Phoenicians, Europa by the Hellenes, Medea by the Hellenes, and Hellen by the Trojans, the last of which led to the legendary Trojan War. In *Soldier of the Mist*, an important character is named Io, and Latro travels on a ship named *Europa*, thereby alluding to two out of four.

Appendix L1-2: The Latro Of Mist

Latro's real name is Lucius. He is from Rome, which at this point in history was a young republic. Latro has forgotten his recent years, but he remembers his childhood: at one point he writes of his parents working the farm and himself carrying away vine cuttings (156); at another time he alludes to an incident when he was "confronted by the crone from the cave on the hill" (234), which woman might be as mundane as a local eccentric, or as mythic as the Cumaean Sibyl.

Because Latro shouts the name "Cassius" as a war cry at the Battle of Thermopylae (*Mist,* 282), there is a good chance he is related to this influential family, since it seems unlikely a non-relative would cry the name of a man recently executed for treason. I refer to Spurius Cassius Viscellinus, who was consul three times, had two triumphs, and wrote the first agrarian law; but from this lofty height he was cast down to ignominy in 485 BC, and his three sons became obscure plebeians. Latro might even be the grandson of Spurius Cassius Viscellinus.

At the end of the novel, Latro finds an eagle standard, that familiar symbol of a Roman legion, but in Latro's era the standards were not limited to eagles. Pliny the Elder lists four other types besides the eagle: the wolf, the ox with a man's head, the horse, and the boar (*Natural History* Book X, 4.5).

Herodotus does not mention any Roman mercenaries in the army of Xerxes, but of all the groups he lists, only one is mysteriously unnamed. He describes only their equipment:

> 76.... [sic] and they had small shields of raw ox-hide, and each man carried two *wolf-hunter's spears.* On their heads they wore helmets of bronze, and to the helmets the ears and horns of an ox were attached, in bronze, and upon them also there were crests; and the lower part of their legs was wrapped round with red-coloured strips of cloth. Among these men there is an Oracle of Ares.

The legs in red cloth may be related to the Roman soldier's red tunic which extended to the knees. Pliny's detail about the "ox with a man's head" standard finds a curious echo with Herodotus's detail on the helmets of the unnamed legion: "to the helmets the ears and horns of an ox were attached, in bronze." Intriguingly, the "Oracle of Ares" detail may even refer to Latro himself after the Battle of Clay.

But in Latro's timeframe it is the early Roman army, and many of the traits we associate with the legion were not yet present in 479 BC: the organization was more like a Greek phalanx, but the basic tactical unit was the 100-man *centuria*. Heavily armed infantry were probably equipped like Greek hoplites; the light infantry were *rorarii* (later called *velites*).

But *velites* (211 to 107 BC) is where it gets interesting: these were the Roman soldiers who wore wolfskin headdresses. They were armed with light javelins and had small round shields. They carried short thrusting swords for use in melee. They were put in the front lines where they could prove themselves and win glory. I am intrigued by the idea that Latro represents a prototype of velite; or that the velites will develop their modes following his example.

A legion would be around 4,000 men, subdivided into a number of centuries. This seems too large for a mercenary group, yet the group, whatever its size, could have an eagle standard.

Then there is Latro's sword, *Falcata*. It is a Celtiberian sword with a curve that makes it more ax-like. This type was crafted from the 5th to the 1st centuries BC, but the Romans famously encountered falcatas for the first time during the Second Punic War (218 to 202 BC), hundreds of years in Latro's future. Latro's *Falcata* is therefore an early example, and it is a mystery as to how he got it. Perhaps his father gave it to him, and this would be a hint that his parents came from the Iberian Peninsula. Perhaps Latro won it as spoils in combat on the Italian Peninsula, presumably against Iberian mercenaries. It seems somewhat less likely that he picked it up while with the Persian army at the other end of the Mediterranean, since, for example, there are no Iberians in the list provided by Herodotus, but it is possible.

Latro's Military History

Latro seems to be in his early to mid-twenties in the year 479 BC, meaning he was born between 505 and 500 BC. Let's say he is 23, so he was born in 502 BC. What sort of large-scale combat might he have experienced on the Italian Peninsula?

He is too young for the Roman-Latin War (498–493 BC), but after that there was annual fighting against Italian tribes the Aequi, the Volsci, or both. This warfare was made up of raids and counter-raids instead of pitched battles.

Latro mentions he was in Persian-controlled Egypt (*Mist*, 184). This could mean he was there during the suppression of the revolt in 484 BC, when our hypothetical Latro would be 18, or that he hired on in Egypt after that revolt was broken, during the four-year build-up for the second invasion of Hellas.

Once in the Persian army, the text shows Latro was at the Battle of Hot Gates, the Battle of Clay, and at the end to the Siege of Sestos. If Latro's group from Rome was like most of the mercenaries hired by Xerxes, they gathered at Asia Minor, crossed the water at Sestos, and marched through Thrace, Macedonia, and Thessaly. A month after Thermopylae, the Persian forces destroyed Athens, and Latro must have been there (his black friend says they were). After the naval Battle of Peace (Salamis), Xerxes retreated to Asia, leaving his general Mardonius to finish the conquest of Hellas with the elite of the army. As Herodotus puts it:

> When he came to Thessaly, then Mardonios chose out for himself first all those Persians who are called "Immortals," except only their commander Hydarnes (for Hydarnes said that he would not be left behind by the king), and after them of the other Persians those who wore cuirasses, and the body of a thousand horse: also the Medes, Sacans, Bactrians and Indians, foot and horsemen

both. These nations he chose in the mass, but from the other allies he selected by few at a time, choosing whose who had fine appearance of those of whom he knew that they had done good service. (Book VIII, 113)

The Battle of Clay (Plataea)

Latro's memory of the battle is sparked by hearing a soldier from the other side talk about it (*Mist,* 183–84). Latro sees Mardonius on his white stallion, surrounded by the Immortals. The trumpets blow, the heralds call to advance (Herodotus says that after a ten-day stand-off, the Greeks were departing from the field, and the Persians gave chase). Latro tries to keep his hundred together, so he is a centurion, but Medes with bows and big wicker shields press through, followed by soldiers of Ethiopia (Nysa) whose bodies are painted red and white. (Herodotus writes that the Medes were there, but he does not state that the Ethiopians were there.)

Then trouble comes as the Greeks stop, turn, and fight.

Latro was wounded in the vicinity of Demeter's temple, near Argiopium, a village around the temple. Herodotus writes that Amonpharetos the Spartan halted at

> the place called Argiopion, where also there stands a temple of the Eleusinian Demeter: and it stayed there for this reason, namely in order that of Amonpharetos and his division should not leave the place where they had been posted, but should remain there, it might be able to come back to their assistance. So Amompharetos and his men were coming up to join them, and the cavalry also of the Barbarians was at the same time beginning to attack them in full force: for the horsemen did on this day as they had been wont to do every day; and seeing the place vacant in which the Hellenes had been posted on the former days, they rode their horses on continually further, and as soon as they came up with them they began to attack them. (Book IX, 57)

The Persian general Mardonius led the way into disaster:

> 63. In the place where Mardonios himself was, riding on a white horse and having about him the thousand best men of the Persians chosen out from the rest, here, I say, they pressed upon their opponents most of all: and so long as Mardonios survived, they held out against them, and defending themselves they cast down many of the Lacedemonians; but when Mardonios was slain and the men who were ranged about his person, which was the strongest portion of the whole army, had fallen, then the others too turned and gave way before the Lacedemonians.

At the death of their commander Mardonius, despair swept through the group near the temple. Latro's line, "The Medes took the spears in their hands and broke them, died" (*Myst,* 184), draws from this passage in Herodotus:

> "Then first there was fighting about the wicker-work shields, and when these had been overturned, after that the fighting was fierce by the side of the temple of Demeter, and so continued for a long time, until at last they came to justling; for the Barbarians would take hold of the spears and break them off." (Book IX, 62)

Here we are, in the territory of the epigraph that started the novel.

Latro's comrade Marcus is dead, one named Umeri is missing, and Latro says, "[W]e should not have gone to Riverland" (*Mist,* 184).

Here is where Lucius fell.

The End and the Aftermath

Artabazos led his Imperial forces away from the battle and began the long march back to Parsa. While Latro lay unconscious on the field, the Imperial survivors who had fought fled back to their fortified camp:

> [T]he Persians and the rest of the throng, having fled for refuge to the palisade, succeeded in getting up to the towers before the Lacedemonians came; and having got

up they strengthened the wall of defence as best they could. Then when the Lacedemonians came up to attack it, there began between them a vigorous fight for the wall: for so long as the Athenians were away, they defended themselves and had much the advantage over the Lacedemonians, since these did not understand the art of fighting against walls; but when the Athenians came up to help them, then there was a fierce fight for the wall, lasting for a long time, and at length by valour and endurance the Athenians mounted up on the wall and made a breach in it, through which the Hellenes poured in. Now the Tegeans were the first who entered the wall, and these were they who plundered the tent of Mardonios, taking, besides the other things which were in it, also the manger of his horse, which was all of bronze and a sight worth seeing. This manger of Mardonios was dedicated by the Tegeans as an offering in the temple of Athene Alea, but all the other things which they took, they brought to the common stock of the Hellenes. The Barbarians however, after the wall had been captured, no longer formed themselves into any close body, nor did any of them think of making resistance, but they were utterly at a loss, as you might expect from men who were in a panic with many myriads of them shut up together in a small space: and the Hellenes were able to slaughter them so that out of an army of thirty myriads, if those four be subtracted which Artabazos took with him in his flight, of the remainder not three thousand men survived. Of the Lacedemonians from Sparta there were slain in the battle ninety-one in all, of the Tegeans sixteen, and of the Athenians two-and-fifty. (Book IX, 70)

Siege of Sestos

Inside the besieged Sestos is the Roman standard bearer along with the few dozen other survivors from Latro's hundred. For them to be there, in Sestos, is something of a puzzle.

The Great King's army had divided a number of times: Xerxes led a retreat after Salamis; Artabazos refused the combat at Plataea and began a retreat from there. But Latro's hundred fought at Clay, so they definitely did not go with Xerxes, and it seems unlikely they went with Artabazos on his long walk to Byzantium. So the remnant of Latro's hundred must have secured immediate boat passage to Sestos, perhaps as an advance guard, only to be trapped there when the siege came.

There is a chance that the standard bearer's name is Umeri, since Latro remarks Umeri was missing (184).

The Soldier Of Nysa

Late in the novel, Latro is reunited with his black friend. Drakaina talks to him in Aram, and she reports that he is from Nysa, south of Riverland. When asked how he learned the language Aram, the black man explains that he was with the Great King's army for three years; how he had gathered 120 soldiers and marched down from Nysa, through Riverland, across the desert to the Crimson Country, and on to the Empire (*Mist*, 300–301). This suggests that he joined in 482 BC. It also implies he learned Aram, presumably Imperial Aramaic, in the Middle East.

The black soldier supposes that remnants of his Nysa group are not in Sestos but "maybe they have gone south with the army" (301). This idea seems based on Artabazos having arrived at Byzantium and sending troops from there before the siege began at Sestos.

Appendix L1-3: Timelines

Timeline for the Second Persian Invasion of Greece
Date: Event
481 BC: The Persian army gathers in Asia Minor in summer and autumn, winters in Sardis.
480 BC (spring): Persian army crosses the Hellespont, then marches through Thrace, Macedonia, and Thessaly.
480 BC (August or September): Battle of Thermopylae (Hot Gates)
480 BC (September): Battle of Salamis (Peace)
480 BC (autumn): Destruction of Athens (Thought)
479 BC (June): Battles of Plataea (Clay) and Mycale
479 BC (autumn): Siege of Sestos ends

Moon Phases
Phase: Chapter
crescent before sunrise: 4.01
waning crescent: 10.01
dark of moon: 22.01

Latro's Timeline

Clay (chapter I) 1 day

road to Hill <break> unknown days

Hill (chapters II, III) 2 days
road (chapters IV to VI) 2 days

marched to Tower Hill <break> unknown days

ship (chapters VII to XI) 2 days
Bay of Peace, Thought (chapters XII to XVI) 1 day
Thought, Advent (chapters XVII to XIX) 1 day

<break> 4 days

Thought (chapters XX to XXII) 2 days
Village (chapters XXIII, XXIV) 1 day
road (chapter XXV) 1 day
Megara (chapters XXVI to XXVIII) 1 day

Tower Hill <break> 1 day
Bearland <break> 1 day

Slave village (chapters XXIX to XXXI) 1 day
Rope (chapter XXXII) 1 day

ship <break> 2 or 3 days

Acheron (chapters XXIII, XXIV) 1 day

ship <break> unknown days sailing
Tower Hill <break> 1 day waiting

Tower Hill/ship/Hot Gates (chapters XXXV to XXXVII) 1 day

ship <break> unknown days

Sestos (chapters XXXVIII to XLIII) 2 days

Appendix L1-4: Earth Goddess Versus Moon Goddess

The earth goddess Demeter and her daughter Kore are locked in a centuries-long battle against the triple Moon goddess Hecate/Artemis/Selene.

Earth
Names
  Mother: Apia, Cybele, Demeter, Earth Mother, Ge, Great Mother, Pig Lady
  Daughter: Maiden, Kore, Queen of the Dead
Sphere
  Mother: Grain, Fertility
  Daughter: Death
Favored Sacrifice
  Mother: Castration, girl sacrifice
Animal Emblems
  Mother: Lion, Wolf

Moon
Names
  Dark Moon: Dark Mother, Enodia, Hecate
  Crescent Moon: Auge, Huntress, Orthia
  Full Moon: Selene
  Triple Goddess: Atimpasa, Trioditis
Sphere: Magic
Sacrifice: Helots, black puppies, boy scourging
Animal Emblems: Serpent, Dog

Latro has been cursed by the earth goddess Demeter. He has a situation similar to that of Odysseus, in trying to return home while being foiled by the gods.

The struggle between Demeter and the Triple Goddess shows up in Oior's telling of the Neurians in Scythia, so the fight is going on in that distant edge of the ancient world, or perhaps it actually started there.

At the major temple in Eleusis, the Maiden tells Latro that the Huntress has taken over the south. Latro sees this as he travels to Rope: the slaves there still worship Ge, but the Rope Maker overlords worship the Huntress.

In the novel, Demeter and her daughter are prepping Pausanias, the regent of Rope. The Maiden gives a dream vision to Pausanias so he will search for Latro; after the sacrifice of a girl and a manhood, Ge promises her followers that Pausanias will become king. Presumably he will do something to support Ge and her people, perhaps a reform of the helot system.

Just as Latro is a human agent of Demeter, the moon goddess has a semi-human agent in Drakaina. First the creature is a serpent woman that helps Latro and tries to get him to sacrifice little Io to her, but Latro refuses. Then when Eurykles seems rather willing and dedicated to the moon goddess, Hecate herself asks Latro to feed him the little snake, beginning a transformation process that results in Drakaina. Drakaina slithers close to Pausanias, driving a wedge between him and his protégé Pasicrates, and even between Pausanias and Queen Gorgo. Supposedly Drakaina will bend Pausanias's path and thereby thwart the will of Demeter. But at the end of the novel, the Maiden tells Latro to make a wolf sacrifice to her, and he does. This comes after the Neurian has already given a mortal wound to Drakaina the serpent-woman. So the semi-human agent has been eliminated, suggesting that the Earth Team is ahead.

Throughout *Mist,* the moon goddess is portrayed as an invader to Hellas. The Slaves of the Rope Makers remember when they were living there, free, and worshipping the earth goddess; then, five hundred years ago (*Mist,* 235), the moon-worshipping overlords came in and turned the place into an open prison. The city that had been ruled by Menelaus and his legendarily beautiful wife Helen during the Golden Age had been degraded into a slave camp, perhaps by the invading Dorians.

Appendix L1-5: The Dionysus Trail

Latro, in addition to being a pawn between the earth goddess and the moon goddess, at times seems to be on the Dionysus trail.

It starts when he joins the celebration of the Kid. Afterwards we learn that the celebration had to do with Dionysus going through the lake to the underworld to rescue his mother. And Latro had worn the mask of a satyr (known as companions to Dionysus), with Hileria taking the role of a nymph.

The priest is telling little Io about the King from Nysa and he seems to take the black man as a divine image or agent.

Some chapters later, Latro sees the old man sleeping under the bush, and he also seems to be a black man from Africa, in addition to being Silenus the god.

Near the end of the novel, Latro learns that his black soldier friend is from Nysa. It starts to look like Latro and his Nysa-friend are similar to the Kid and Silenus.

Pondering on how Latro might be like Dionysus leads to a few strange bits. For example, Dionysus is of uncertain origin, sometimes Thracian, other times Greek (Latro's origin is mysterious). Dionysus is often described as being "twice-born," having been killed and reborn, or having been conceived in a woman's womb yet brought to term in a god's body (Latro is "born again" because he has lost his memory, and Apollo helps him along, almost like a second father).

But in the main, Dionysus is a god of the vine, god of wine, god of ritual madness, and god of religious ecstasy, none of which seems to apply to Latro.

L1-6: Apollo Prophecy Checklist

When Latro is at the Temple of Apollo (*Mist,* Chapter III), the god says to him, "Only the solitary may see the gods. For the rest, every god is the Unknown God" (11). After a bit of conversation, Apollo says:

> A. "I prophesy that though you will wander far in search of your home, you will not find it until you are farthest from it.
>
> B. Once only, you will sing as men sang in the Age of Gold to the playing of the gods.
>
> C. Long after, you will find what you seek in the dead city.
>
> D. "Though healing is mine, I cannot heal you, nor would I if I could; by the shrine of the Great Mother you fell, to a shrine of hers you must return.
>
> E. Then she will point the way, and in the end the wolf's tooth will return to her who sent it
>
> F. Look beneath the sun...." (11–12).

The version of the pythoness goes like this:
    1. Look under the sun, if you would see!
    2. Sing! Make sacrifice to me!
    3. But you must cross the narrow sea.
    4. The wolf that howls has wrought you woe!
    5. To that dog's mistress you must go!
    6. Her hearth burns in the room below.
    7. I send you to the God Unseen!
    8. Whose temple lies in Death's terrene!
    9. There you shall learn why He's not seen.
    10. Sing then, and make the hills resound!
    11. King, nymph, and priest shall gather round!
    12. Wolf, faun, and nymph, spellbound. (15)

The Apollo and Pythoness lines seem related at points:

A/Pythoness
A
B/2, 10–11
C
D/5
E/6
F/1

A few of the lines seem fulfilled:

A (Chapter fulfilled in Mist)
A
B (V: king of Nysa, nymph Hilaeira, priest Pindaros)
C
D (XIX: meet the Maiden)
E (XIX: meet the Maiden)
F

Appendix L1-7: Latro And The Gods

A list of supernatural details.

- Demeter curses Latro with the "wolf tooth" (before ch. I).
- Latro prays to Asopus, who blesses his sword (ch. I).
- He prays to an Asopus fountain, which leads to cash and a trip to Apollo (ch. II).
- Apollo gives Latro words of advice (ch. II).
- Latro becomes a one-night satyr for Dionysus. Hilaeira is affected (between chapters III and IV).
- The Huntress comes looking for Dionysus but finds Latro bathing in the lake (ch. IV, as the goddess tells it later in ch. XXI).
- Latro touches Silenus, and helots see him (ch. V).
- The snake woman urges Latro to select a victim, but he resists (ch. VI; end of Part I).
- At least two of the four foreign bowmen suspect Latro is a Neurian, probably misreading the "wolf tooth" as the werewolf curse, and they plan to kill him (ch. XI).
- Latro sees Hades and shades of bowman Spu and sailor Kekrops (ch. XI).
- At the graveyard Latro touches a corpse, gets a message from Hades (ch. XVI).
- At Demeter's Temple, the miracle of the statue means that Hilaeira will become a high priestess, a boon to Demeter (ch. XVIII).
- The Maiden meets Latro (ch. XIX, end of Part II).
- After Latro repairs her statue (ch. XII), the dove goddess visits him, then Kalleos propositions him (ch. XX, beginning of Part III).
- Moon goddess tells him to select a victim, and he does (ch. XXII).
- Heracles gives Latro wrestling tips (ch. XXIII).
- Latro sees Aesculapius (ch. XXV).

- The Maiden shows Latro to Pausanius in a dream (ch. XXVII).
- Latro sees earth goddess, touches her (ch. XXXI).
- Latro sees expression of Huntress statue (ch. XXXII, end of part III).
- At Acheron sacrifice, Latro sees shades of Cleomenes and Eurykles (ch. XXXIII).
- Latro meets Thoe, daughter of Nereus (ch. XXXVI).
- Latro gets combat help from shades of Odysseus and Achilles (ch. XLII).
- The Maiden tells Latro to make a wolf sacrifice (ch. XLI), and he does (ch. XLIII, end Part IV).

SOLDIER OF ARETE

Soldier Of Arete

Edition cited: Tor (hb), ISBN 93185-9, September 1989, 354 pp.

Dedication:

> This book
> is dedicated
> to the old colonel,
> the most underrated
> of ancient authors
> and the least heeded:
> Xenophon the Athenian

Commentary: Xenophon the Athenian (c. 431–c. 354 BC) was an ancient Greek historian, philosopher, and soldier. He wrote a number of books, the most germane in this context being *Anabasis,* about his time as a Greek mercenary leading the Ten Thousand hired by Cyrus the Younger in 401 BC for a failed campaign to claim the Persian throne.

The selection of Xenophon was a surprise for history-minded readers who anticipated that Thucydides would be next, since Thucydides picked up the history after the fall of Sestos. The sequence of historians goes Herodotus, Thucydides, and Xenophon.

Epigraph:

> And there came one to Xenophon as he was offering sacrifice, and said, "Gryllus is dead." And Xenophon took off the garland that was on his head, but ceased not his sacrifice. Then the messenger said, "His death was noble." And Xenophon returned the garland to his head again; and it is the tale that he shed no tears, but said, "I knew that I begat him mortal."
>
> —Diogenes Laertius

This quote is from *The Lives and Opinions of Eminent Philosophers,* Book II, section X. It sketches the Athenian losses at the Second Battle of Mantinea in 362 BC, but the quote clearly shows the "arete" (excellence, virtue) alluded to in the novel's title.

Foreword: (ix–x) Gene Wolfe warns about the fragmentary nature of this new scroll, due to water damage.
- A gap of a week or more after the party left Pactye
- Loss of a considerable portion with the arrival of the Europa at Piraeus
- A third hiatus due to morbid depression after manumission at Sparta

Notes on ancient cavalry. Notes on Amazons as historical.

Part 1

Chapter 1: I Will Make a New Beginning

1.01: (3–5) Latro starts a new scroll. He is with little Io and the black man in Sestos. Io's hair is long and dark. The season is winter.

1.02: (5–11) In the evening, something "quite unusual" happens.

Hypereides has Latro come with him to visit the prisoner Artaÿctes. His main point is to ask Artaÿctes if Oeobazus was in the escape group from Sestos. Artaÿctes says he was, with the town Pactye as the goal. Hypereides vows to have Artaÿctes and his son Artembares spared.

Latro is sent to fetch wine. On the way he sees the chariot of the sun. He returns with the wine and Artaÿctes tries to bribe him, but Hypereides returns with salted pilchards which he puts on the brazier.

The pilchards begin flopping as if alive.

Artaÿctes says it is a message for him. He makes an offer to pay a kingly sum for his crimes. Hypereides takes the message that night.

Having written that, Latro plans to return immediately to the citadel.

Herodotus: The historian tells the portent of the fish in Book IX:

> 120. Then, it is said by the men of the Chersonese, as one of those who guarded them [Artaÿctes and his son] was frying dried fish, a portent occurred as follows,—the dried fish when laid upon the fire began to leap and struggle just as if they were fish newly caught: and the others gathered round and were marvelling at the portent, but Artaÿctes seeing it called to the man who was frying the fish and said: "Stranger of Athens, be not at all afraid of this portent, seeing that it has not appeared for thee but for me. Protesilaos who dwells at Elaius signifies thereby that though he is dead and his body is dried like those fish, yet he has power given him by the gods to exact vengeance

from the man who does him wrong. Now therefore I desire to impose this penalty for him,—that in place of the things which I took from the temple I should pay down a hundred talents to the god, and moreover as ransom for myself and my son I will pay two hundred talents to the Athenians, if my life be spared."

Geography: The Thracian Chersonese (the modern peninsula of Gallipoli) forms the European shore of Helle's Sea. In ancient times its Greek colonies were protected by the Long Wall, a barrier built across the narrowest part of the peninsula to prevent invasion by the Apsinthii, a Thracian tribe. Herodotus wrote that the wall was between Cardia and Pactye (VI, 36).

Chapter 2: Artaÿctes Dies

2.01: (11–18) In the morning Hypereides and Latro go to see the execution. Hypereides tries to explain away the pilchard portent. Artaÿctes's son looks about fourteen, "a bit older than Io" (12).

Xanthippos of Thought arrives. His speech to the crowd riles them up against Hill. He alludes to the Battle of Clay, and how Hill had sided with the Great King there.

Artaÿctes's son is killed by stoning, then Artaÿctes is crucified.

The cables for the incredible bridge of boats are in Sestos. The builder was Oeobazus. The job is to get him and take him to Thought.

When Latro and his black friend return to the house they are staying at, they find that little Io is missing.

Geography: "First Sea" is the Aegean Sea (by way of "Archepelagos," the earlier name for this body of water); "Helle's Sea" is the Hellespont, now the Dardanelles.

The Pontoon Bridges of Xerxes are said to have crossed Helle's Sea from Abydos on the Asian side to Sestos on the Thracian Chersonese. The distance, according to Herodotus, was seven stadia (around 1,300 meters or 1,400 yards). The orientation was more north/south than east/west.

Herodotus: The fate of Artaÿctes is given in Book IX, where the Athenian had promised to deliver the offer of a princely cash settlement,

> but he did not prevail upon the commander Xanthippos; for the people of Elaius desiring to take vengeance for Protesilaos asked that he might be put to death, and the inclination of the commander himself tended to the same conclusion. They brought him therefore to that headland to which Xerxes made the passage across, or as some say to the hill which is over the town of Madytos, and there they nailed him to boards and hung him up; and they stoned his son to death before the eyes of Artaÿctes himself. (Book IX, 120)

Chapter 3: The Mantis

3.01: (19–25) Latro and the black man figure that little Io had followed to see the execution. They go to the market to buy the cloaks Hypereides wanted. They discover Hypereides had already bought a red cloak, which is a mystery.

They find Io at the crucifixion with a man who has a wooden foot. He is Hegesistratus, from the Isle of Zakunthios. He is also from Elis, and little Io says she and Latro visited Elis on the way to Acheron (25).

Hegesistratus has a talent for languages and translates the black man's name as "Seven Lions."

They bring Hegesistratus to stay at the house they are at. Latro wants to know his opinion of his sword.

Phoenician Words: zlh (cheap), sel (jackal). Aramaic.

Chapter 4: Favorable Auspices

4.01: (26–33) Later that day, Latro has a weird episode where he approaches Hegesistratus with his sword. Hegesistratus disarms him and they examine the case of possession. He talks of divinity as transmitted like a disease.

Hypereides arrives. Hegesistratus introduces himself and Hypereides knows he was the mantis of Mardonius at Clay. They work out this complication, since Hypereides was on the other side. Hypereides says the Assembly of Thought wanted to punish Hill for siding with the Great King by leveling the city and selling its population into slavery; Rope vetoed this.

Latro shows Hypereides the cloaks they purchased but he refrains from asking about the red cloak they had heard about.

Little Io urges Latro to write. Hegesistratus interrupts.

Hegesistratus tries to break the charm put on Latro by Tisamenus of Elis (*Mist,* chapter XXIV), whose family has been rivals of his family since the Golden Age.

Herodotus: The historian mentions the fate of Thebes after the Battle of Clay (Plataea) in Book IX:

> 86. When the Hellenes had buried their dead at Plataia, forthwith they determined in common council to march upon Thebes and to ask the Thebans to surrender those who had taken the side of the Medes, and among the first of them Timagenides and Attaginos, who were leaders equal to the first; and if the Thebans did not give them up, they determined not to retire from the city until they had taken it. Having thus resolved, they came accordingly on the eleventh day after the battle and began to besiege the Thebans, bidding them give the men up: and as the Thebans refused to give them up, they began to lay waste their land and also to attack their wall.
>
> 87. So then, as they did not cease their ravages, on the twentieth day Timagenides spoke as follows to the Thebans: "Thebans, since it has been resolved by the Hellenes not to retire from the siege until either they have taken Thebes or ye have delivered us up to them, now therefore let not the land of Boeotia suffer any more for our sakes, but if they desire to have money and are demanding our surrender as a colour for this, let us give them money taken out of the treasury of the State; for we took the side of the Medes together with the State and not by ourselves alone: but if they are making the siege truly in order to get us into their hands, then we will give ourselves up for trial." In this it was thought that he spoke very well and seasonably, and the Thebans forthwith sent

a herald to Pausanias offering to deliver up the men.

88. After they had made an agreement on these terms, Attaginos escaped out of the city; and when his sons were delivered up to Pausanias, he released them from the charge, saying that the sons had no share in the guilt of taking the side of the Medes. As to the other men whom the Thebans delivered up, they supposed that they would get a trial, and they trusted moreover to be able to repel the danger by payment of money; but Pausanias, when he had received them, suspecting this very thing, first dismissed the whole army of allies, and then took the men to Corinth and put them to death there. These were the things which happened at Plataia and at Thebes.

Chapter 5: Our Ship

5.01: (33–35) Out from Sestos onto Helle's Sea. Hegesistratus seems ill, but little Io won't tell Latro any details. Notes on Latro and Seven Lions as oarsmen.

Greek: Kybernetes means "steersman."

5.02: (35) Seven Lions goes and comes back, will not tell Latro why.

5.03: (35–40) They land on shore. Little Io says they are traveling to Pactye, where the wall is.

At night Latro sees a woman who is the bride of a tree. After sacrifice, she offers him a glimpse of his fields. He sees an old man plowing, and a garden, a vineyard, and a low white house. At the house Latro sees a creature neither ape nor bear, the Lares he had remembered before. His mother is napping, so she sees him and calls him Lucius.

After the vision he lies with the dryad, whose name is Elata.

Then Latro hears hunting dogs coming closer. A stag comes and goes.

Myth: The Lares domestici were guardian deities in ancient Roman religion. It is not known how they were represented in the days of the early republic, but in later eras they were depicted as boys in rustic clothing.

Onomastics: Elata's name means "pine" (*Arete* glossary).

Chapter 6: The Nymph

6.01: (41–49) The hounds come, followed by the Huntress and her retinue. The hunt is interrupted by this discovery of lovers. The Huntress gives a task to Latro, Hegesistratus, and the nymph Elata: she says they will soon meet a queen who has a strong protector, and the Huntress means to use him to flush a boar. They must aid this queen. "But when the moment comes, the slut must lose. It will be at my brother's house" (43). She says, "My queen must win in order that the prince may be destroyed—and thus this queen must not win" (44). "You bring victory, Latro, so you must drive for my prince" (44).

In exchange she promises to return Latro to living friends. She grants Elata to Hegesistratus until he brings her back to this tree.

In quick order Elata lies with Hegesistratus and then with one of Acetes's shieldmen.

Hegesistratus tells about the Huntress and her twin, the Destroyer. She is daughter of the Thunderer.

Io reports a large creature moving among the trees. The men say it is probably a cow.

Latro talks about the boy on the ship but Io and Hegesistratus insist there is not a boy on the ship. Dawn comes as Latro finishes writing.

Mystery: Is it a coincidence that the Huntress arrives after the nymph has been naughty? While there was a stag, this might be a misdirection: the suggestion is that the prey she was coursing is the large creature little Io was frightened by. What is it, and where did it come from?

Chapter 7: Oeobazus Is Among the Apsinthians

7.01: (49–56) They are at the city Pactye on Helle's Sea. Latro senses he is close to fulfilling a bit of the oracular verse relating to the "narrow sea."

Latro estimates little Io is eleven or twelve years old.

Hegesistratus has heard that Oeobazus is with a tribe. To get more information, he will perform at a sacred grove of Itys.

Latro speaks a bit of the Crimson Men language.

Buying fire for the rite, Latro learns Itys had been eaten by his father.

Phoenician Terms: bahut (hello), uhuya (my brother), sisuw (a big animal), bun/nucir (boy).

Commentary: Little Io seems to be growing rapidly. When first seen, she came to Latro's waist. Next she was up to his ribs, which seems like three or four inches.

Chapter 8: The Europa Sails at Dawn

8.01: (56–62) At the sacred grove, they light the fire. Hegesistratus tells the story of Itys. He instructs Latro to ask the ghost boy about Oeobazus.

Hegesistratus tells Hypereides that Hegesistratus, Latro, Seven Lions, Io, and Elata must track Oeobazus in Thrace. So the party will split in two, as the ship will pursue some piracy on the Crimson Men.

Latro thinks Hegesistratus is lying and plans to kill him.

History: The Great King is Xerxes.

Geography: Parsa is Persia, the Empire.

Myth: Itys was the son of a Thracian king. The sad story of Philomela, whom the king had raped and made mute, is made more horrible by her revenge upon the king's son, her nephew Itys, whom she killed and secretly served as food to his father.

8.02: (62–63) Io offers herself to Latro, but he refuses because of her young age. Later she weeps at the prospect of being returned to be a temple slave at Hill.

End of Part 1

Synopsis of Part 1: From Sestos to Pactye (Chapter 1 to 8)

Artaÿctes's son is stoned, then Artaÿctes is crucified. Hegesistratus joins the group and Latro tries to kill him. The new task is to find Oeobazus, builder of the bridge across Helle's Sea, and they set out for Pactye.

Along the way, Latro encounters a nymph, then the Huntress. Elata the dryad joins the group.

At Pactye they divine clues that Oeobazus is in Thrace. The party splits in two, with the ship looking to do some piracy. Latro still wants to kill Hegesistratus.

Part 2

Chapter 9: Elata Says

9.01: (67–73) Latro sees Elata dancing in the morning with two river nymphs. The river is the Mela, the edge of Apsinthian territory.

Latro had seen a big man on a big horse with a hunting lion beside him.

The plan is to meet the *Europa* at the queen's great temple at the mouth of the Hebrus.

Latro finds tracks of a lion, but not of the big horse.

After the second meal (evening), they are met by nine riders.

Combat erupts, but then a female cavalry group storms through.

Latro and Hegesistratus use first aid on a fallen woman. They think she will die.

Geography: "Melas" is the name of several rivers, but the Thracian one, "now called *Saldatti* or *Scheher-Su,* falling into a deep bay ... which is bounded on the east by the shore of the Thracian Chersonesus. The modern name of the bay is the gulf of *Saros*" (William Smith, *Dictionary of Greek and Roman Geography, Volume 2*).

Hebrus (or Maritza) is the principal river of Thrace.

Myth: The decapitated head of Orpheus was kept afloat by Hebrus the river god.

Dionysus: Orpheus had been killed by female followers of Dionysus.

9.02: (73) Hegesistratus talks with one of the women long into the night.

Chapter 10: The Amazons

10.01: (74–75) Hegesistratus learns the women are the Amazons. Pharetra is the wounded one. "Pharetra" is the closest approximation Latro can make to her name.

Herodotus: The historian discusses Amazons (Book IV, 110–

117).

10.02: (75–77) The combined group enters a Thracian town. The highest Thracians have tattooed cheeks and gold rings. Latro makes notes on Thracian equipment and Amazon equipment.

Latro perhaps is blond, since he notes of Pharetra, "Her hair is nearly the color of my own, though I think more touched with red" (75).

10.03: (77) The town is Cobrys, the king's name is Kotys. Latro's party is being guarded by Thracians. Latro plans on sneaking around later.

Geography: Cobrys was a coastal Greek town in ancient Thrace, on the Thracian Chersonesus. It was a trading post of Cardia, a city of the Long Wall.

Onomastics: "Kotys" was "the name of numerous Thracian Kings" (*Arete* glossary). For example, Kotys I (Odrysian) ruled 383–359 BC.

Myth: "Kotys" was a Thracian goddess, thought by Greeks to be an aspect of Persephone. Her cult was similar to the cult of the goddess Bendis, the Thracian Artemis. This ambiguity is especially charged in Latro's story, which, in *Mist*, at least, involves a struggle between the Maiden (Persephone) and the Huntress (Artemis).

10.04: (77–81) Latro asks Hegesistratus to tell his future. Little Io wants the same, too. To do this, Hegesistratus uses a mirror to look at the stars.

Hegesistratus says Nike accompanies Latro always, and the Destroyer smiles upon him, but then Hegesistratus sees his own death and drops the mirror.

Hegesistratus says Latro might see Nike behind him in a mirror, which matches a detail a few chapters earlier, when Latro polished Hypereides's armor and saw "a tall woman with a shining face stood behind me" (Chapter 7, 51).

Hegesistratus says Latro will travel far. He sees the Lady of

Thought and the Huntress playing a game, meaning each will use Latro in the game if she can.

The Amazon queen is Hippephode. She asks if Hegesistratus saw the War God. The answer is no. She asked since she thinks Latro has his virtues, "arete."

The Thracians wear foxskin caps.

Before Latro lies down, a rider with a dog joins the guards.

Myth: Nike, the personification of victory, is often depicted as a miniature in the hand of Athena and Zeus. The Boundary Stone, "patron of travelers" (79), is Hermes.

Onomastics: Hippephode's name means "cavalry charge" (79, and *Arete* glossary).

Commentary: In *Mist* the goddess conflict was between Demeter and the moon goddess. Hegesistratus sees a game between Athena and the moon goddess. This suggests a new one-on-one fight, or a two-against-one fight, or even a three-way fight.

Chapter 11: Ares and Others

11.01: (81–89) Latro wakes in the night and sneaks around to learn about the town. He finds a Hellene householder, Cleton, who asks Latro if the Great King is coming back, because last time his army bought everything Cleton had and paid well, too. He also saw Hegesistratus then, which makes it more likely it was on the army's outward track toward Hellas rather than the retreat.

Cleton will help the group.

Latro learns that the god Pleistorus is the Thracian Ares. He tries to find his way to Pleistorus's temple.

Along the way he is caught up by a dancing procession of five, including nymph Elata, but it is heading from the temple of the Mother of the Gods. King Kotys passes.

Back at the camp, Latro plunges his sword into sleeping Hegesistratus. It was a trick, and his friends make him prisoner.

Herodotus: The historian writes of the Thracians, "of the gods they worship only Ares and Dionysos and Artemis" (Book

V, 7). He later identifies Pleistorus as a god native to the Apsinthian Thracians (Book IX, 119).

Myth: Pleistorus is "[a] name under which the War God is worshipped in Thrace" (*Arete* glossary).

Chapter 12: We Will Fight

12.01: (90–99) Hegesistratus tells Latro how he lost his foot. His ancestral city Elis was seized by Rope Makers while he was visiting. They took him to Rope. They promised to kill him the next morning, but left him with a dagger to kill himself instead. They had done the same with their own King Cleomenes. But Hegesistratus amputated his foot and escaped.

Back in the Thracian present, King Kotys sends them an ultimatum. They consider carefully and decide they will fight, beginning that night.

Herodotus: The historian tells of Hegesistratus in Book IX, beginning with the fact that he was the mantis for the losing (Persian) side, then going into his amazing personal history:

> 37, and [the Persian general]... [had] as diviner Hegesistratos an Eleian and the most famous of the Telliadai, whom before these events the Spartans had taken and bound, in order to put him to death, because they had suffered much mischief from him. He then being in this evil case, seeing that he was running a course for his life and was likely moreover to suffer much torment before his death, had done a deed such as may hardly be believed. Being made fast on a block bound with iron, he obtained an iron tool, which in some way had been brought in, and contrived forthwith a deed the most courageous of any that we know: for having first calculated how the remaining portion of his foot might be got out of the block, he cut away the flat of his own foot, and after that, since he was guarded still by warders, he broke through the wall and so ran away to Tegea, travelling during the nights and in the daytime entering a wood and resting there; so that, though the Lacedemonians searched for him in full force, he arrived at Tegea on the third night; and the Lacedemonians were possessed by great wonder both at

his courage, when they saw the piece of the foot that was cut off lying there, and also because they were not able to find him. So he at that time having thus escaped them took refuge at Tegea, which then was not friendly with the Lacedemonians; and when he was healed and had procured for himself a wooden foot, he became an open enemy of the Lacedemonians.

Chapter 13: We Await the Attack

13.01: (100–107) Hegesistratus tells Latro about the feud within his family, between the sons of Tellias and the sons of Clytias, then about his relative Tisamenus and his ambition to win at the Pythic Games. Hegesistratus shows how Tisamenus used two spells on Latro, one to make him kill Hegesistratus, and another to make him forget Tisamenus had ordered this. He also explains that the charade with the boots was his own spell to counteract the evil spell.

Herodotus: The historian tells of Tisamenus in Book IX. While he does not mention kinship between Tisamenus and Hegesistratus (aside from both being soothsayers from Elis), he does detail how Delphic oracles led Tisamenus to believe he would have incredible victory at the games:

> 33. When all had been drawn up by nations and by divisions, then on the next day they offered sacrifice on both sides. For the Hellenes Tisamenos the son of Antiochos was he who offered sacrifice, for he it was who accompanied this army as diviner. This man the Lacedemonians had made to be one of their own people, being an Eleian and of the race of the Iamidai: for when Tisamenos was seeking divination at Delphi concerning issue, the Pythian prophetess made answer to him that he should win five of the greatest contests. He accordingly, missing the meaning of the oracle, began to attend to athletic games, supposing that he should win contests of athletics; and he practised for the "five contests" and came within one fall of winning a victory at the Olympic games, being set to contend with Hieronymos of Andros. The Lacedemonians however perceived that the oracle given to Tisamenos had reference

not to athletic but to martial contests, and they endeavoured to persuade Tisamenos by payment of money, and to make him a leader in their wars together with the kings of the race of Heracles.

After being recruited by Rope, Tisamenus was their mantis at the Battle of Plataea (Clay):

> 36. This Tisamenos was acting now as diviner for the Hellenes in the Plataian land, being brought by the Spartans. Now to the Hellenes the sacrifices were of good omen if they defended themselves only, but not if they crossed the Asopos and began a battle.

History: Elis had three mantic families, the sons of Iamus, Klytus, and Tellias. Tisamenus was an Iamidai (not a Klytidai, as Wolfe suggests); Hegesistratus was "the most famous of the Telliadai."

Chapter 14: In the Cave of the Mother of the Gods

14.01: (107–108) They are holed up in a cave.

14.02: (108–14) Back to the day before: Cleton reports that he talked to King Kotys but got nowhere. Then he went to the temple and discovered they are holding Oeobazus prisoner to sacrifice him.

Cleton tells about the curtain at the temple. It shows the god Pleistorus riding his horse, with his lion running beside him, against Zalmoxis as a boar in the corner.

Cleton gives the geneology of King Kotys: descended from Tereus, who was son of Pleistorus. Pleistorus is son of Kotytto, Thracian Rhea, and sometimes he is her lover, too.

The sacrifice is probably spurred by the oracle of Orpheus's head in Lesbos during the spring.

Cleton says the Apsinthii will attack that night.

Latro's group prepares to move first.

Myth: Regarding a goddess and her son that is sometimes her lover, too, this sounds a lot like the pattern with Demeter and Iacchus (who is connected with Dionysus). "*Kotytto*—A name under which Gaea is worshipped in Thrace" (*Arete* glossary). "*Orpheus*—A shaman killed by the Thracian women; his head was cast into the Hebrus, still pronouncing the name of his lost wife" (*Arete* glossary).

Chapter 15: I Would Go Now

15.01: (115) In the cave, Latro decides to sneak out in the night, through the cave's other mouth. He will go to the temple.

15.02: (115–24) Back to the day before: Hegesistratus explains the oracular verse to Latro and little Io. Three gods are mentioned: the War God; the Huntress; and the Sun. The locals watched all year: in summer the Great King's forces streamed through Apsinthia in retreat, yet the oracle had no bearing; but now the arrival of the Amazons seems to fit. King Kotys fears for his life. He moved up the sacrifice schedule and intends to strike first, when the moon is high.

Latro's group ambushes the Apsinthii on the road. Latro seizes the king. In fleeing pursuit, Latro drops the king. They retreat into a sacred cave where they kill the castrated priest who attacks.

Little Io has a sword given to her by Queen Hippephode, a sword belonging to an Amazon who was killed before they met Latro's group.

Latro writes chapters 14 and 15 before going to sleep.

Myth: The Orphic verses relate to Pleistorus (Ares), Bendis (Artemis), and her twin (Apollo).

Commentary: Hegesistratus establishes that the retreating army came through Apsinthia in summer.

Chapter 16: The Horses of the Sun

16.01: (124–32) The Thracians invade the cave before dawn but are beaten. As spoils, Latro is given a mail shirt and a helmet.

Latro sneaks out during the truce, going deeper into the cave. After a while he hears two lions, who made their den in the other cave mouth.

He reads the scroll, from "I Would Go Now" (chapter 15). He sees how the oracle statements about the ox and the child have been fulfilled. (The "ox" being the castrated priest who attacked them; the "child" being little Io who now rides like an Amazon.)

As he walks toward the lions, things shift. The stalagmite seems like a temple's column. Things keep shifting.

He emerges to find four lions and a lioness in human form. She is the earth goddess Cybele, and she has Latro stand in her silver chariot. She says, "You do not recall your meeting with the usurper, and that is my doing, though you do not recall that either" (131). ("Usurper" here being the one who promised Latro last: the Huntress.)

The Amazons came to Thrace to buy sacred horses from the Temple of the Sun.

Cybele sends Latro on a mission to get the horses and bring them to the cave.

Myth: Cybele's chariot is drawn by four lions, so this scene is mythologically accurate.

Apollo Prophecy: Jeremy Crampton points out that Cybele says "Look under the sun" (132), an echo of Apollo's advice to Latro ("Some Greek Themes in Gene Wolfe's Latro novels").

Chapter 17: Sworn Before All the Gods

17.01: (133–34) Negotiations to exchange twenty-one horses for Oeobazus and to purchase four horses.

17.02: (134–37) Back to the action before: Latro follows Cybele's instructions. She had promised three helpers, and he meets one of her lions, then Pharetra the Amazon, and both join him. Then Elata rides up with a colt. Latro takes the colt and the task is quickly done.

They take twenty-five horses to the cave. Boy Polos joins.

The Thracian herdsmen report to their king that the sacred herd was taken by Pleistorus.

Odysseus: Latro's Horses of the Sun adventure bears some resemblance to the "Cattle of the Sun" episode of Book XII in

The Odyssey, where Odysseus is warned not to molest the Cattle of Helios, but his men eat them anyway. Back at sea they are blasted by lightning for this, and Odysseus alone survives to swim to Calypso's island.

Heracles: The hero deals with special horses, the Mares of Diomedes, in his eighth labor. This adventure was set in Thrace.

17.03: (137–38) A bundle of firewood holds arrows smuggled to them from Cleton.

17.04: (138–41) Little Io is concerned that Elata will betray them, but Latro reasons that she was one of the three helpers Cybele sent, and so she would not.

Io is puzzled about Pharetra, who seemed near death when they first met her, yet rose up to fight and fight again.

Latro studies his scroll and sees Elata is a nymph.

17.05: (141) Hegesistratus divines that Oeobazus is still alive.

Chapter 18: Pharetra Is Dead

18.01: (141–43) Latro wakes up beside sleeping Pharetra. The Amazon Hippostizein leads him to stand night guard at the cave mouth. After a while, Hegesistratus goes outside for a time.

In the morning, Pharestra is killed in the surprise attack by peltists.

Onomastics: Hippostizein means "trooper" (*Arete* glossary).

18.02: (143–44) Two Thracian lords come calling for a truce. They claim the peltists were acting on their own. Latro lets one go back and keeps the other as hostage.

18.03: (144–48) Little Io says Polos has talent with horses. Latro tries to figure out whose child he is. Polos shows the little gold coins he got from the dead men. Io says the Thracians call Latro the hero, meaning that Pleistorus is inside of him.

Commentary: "Thracian Rider" is the name given to a recurring motif of a horseman in art from about the 3rd century BC to the 3rd century AD. The rider is shown as a hunter on horseback, accompanied by a hunting dog or a lion, attacking a boar. Inscriptions identify the rider as "Heros," that is, hero.

This figure that Latro has seen since crossing the river into Apsinthia is clearly the Thracian Rider.

Chapter 19: My Duel with the King

19.01: (149–56) Latro's group goes to the Pleistorus temple. Oeobazus is produced.

Queen Hippephode selects four horses and pays gold.

Then King Kotys forces a mounted duel with Latro.

As they charge towards each other, something changes. Suddenly all are fighting, even Thracians against each other. Then Hegesistratus urges Latro to run clear.

Latro catches up with Io. At a farmhouse they use one of the small gold coins they had taken as spoils from bodies in the cave. Polos joins them with three horses, one of them Latro's. Then Cleton joins, with word that Kotys is dead, Prince Thamyris rules the city, and Rope Makers have arrived, looking for Oeobazus and Latro's group.

Chapter 20: Raskos

20.01: (157–64) A wounded man named Raskos comes in before sunrise. Polos is very agitated by him. The farmer's name is Olepys.

A mourning woman comes next, and she wants the farmer to come to the funeral of her husband Raskos. His ghost had just preceded them.

Polos tells Latro about the duel, how Kotys ran and his people killed him for that.

The group heads out, looking for Hegesistratus.

Commentary: "*Raskos*—A peltist killed by Latro" (*Arete* glossary).

Chapter 21: The Strategist from Rope

21.01: (165–66) Latro, little Io, Polos, nymph Elata, and Amazon Badizoe are in a village. The villagers say the leader from

Rope demands any foreigners to be handed over. Prince Thamyris and the loyalist faction hold the palace.

Latro's group joins Badizoe in searching for the Amazons and Hegesistratus.

Onomastics: Badizoe means "slow march/walk" (*Arete* glossary).

21.02: (166–70) Latro drinks too much and tries to molest sleeping Elata, but the hills become uneasy, and the horses begin speaking, so he reads his scroll.

He heaps wood on the fire, which brings the boy from Susa to pray at the fire. His name is Artembares.

Latro talks to him about Ahura Mazda.

Artembares tells Latro how, back at Sestos, Latro had tried to free the boy and his father Artaÿctes (a version quite different from the text of Chapter 1; or, more accurately, it gives a new Chapter 1.5, describing what happened when Latro went back alone). Artembares points the direction to Oeobazus.

Polos wakes up and gets very agitated about Artembares.

21.03: (170–72) When the others wake, Latro tells them, and they follow a young red stallion to a farm where Hegesistratus and Oeobazus are hiding. While Latro sharpens his sword, Oeobazus walks up, thanks him, and shakes his hand.

A chariot arrives, accompanied by Amazons. Riding in the chariot is a Rope Maker who seems to recognize them with joy.

Chapter 22: That's Where We Camped

22.01: (172–81) The group is passing by the previous camp they had shared with the Amazons in the rye field. The Amazons have already left them after the first meal (noon), escorted by Thracian guards to the Hebrus, western border of Apsinthia.

Latro is writing at a house back in Cobrys. It belonged to one of the lords who sided with Thamyris. Acetes, the commander of the soldiers on Hyperides's ship, is the one posing as a strategist from Rope.

Oeobazus says that, years before, he met a tribe who believe the War God is Ahura Mazda in disguise.

Oeobazus relates the tragic loss of his three sons. Then he goes out to ride at night before sleep. Polos follows him.

Hegesistratus tells the tale of Captain Hubrias and the White Isle: Two years before the war, the ghost of Achilles appeared on a White Isle off the mouth of the Ister and tasked Hubrias to bring him a certain slave woman, the last of Priam's line. Hubrias found her, bought her, and brought her to the ghost, who was with another ghost, a beautiful woman. Achilles promised him great reward, and his life has been charmed ever since. Yet as he was departing that shore, the ghosts began torturing the girl, and they tore her apart.

Acetes begins telling of the necromancy he witnessed in Athens, but he is interrupted by a pounding at the door. Upon opening it, they find Oeobazus and Polos aiding a fat old man with a head injury.

Herodotus: The tragedy of Oeobazus losing his sons is similar to an incident depicted by the historian in Book VII:

> 38. Then as he was leading forth his army on its march, Pythios the Lydian, being alarmed by the appearance in the heavens and elated by the gifts which he had received, came to Xerxes, and said as follows: "Master, I would desire to receive from thee a certain thing at my request, which, as it chances, is for thee an easy thing to grant, but a great thing for me, if I obtain it." Then Xerxes, thinking that his request would be for anything rather than that which he actually asked, said that he would grant it, and bade him speak and say what he desired. He then, when he heard this, was encouraged, and spoke these words: "Master, I have, as it chances, five sons, and it is their fortune to be all going together with thee on the march against Hellas. Do thou, therefore, O king, have compassion upon me, who have come to so great an age, and release from serving in the expedition one of my sons, the eldest, in order that he may be caretaker both of myself and of my wealth: but the other four take with thyself, and after thou hast accomplished that which thou hast in thy mind, mayest thou have a safe return home."

39. Then Xerxes was exceedingly angry and made answer with these words: "Thou wretched man, dost thou dare, when I am going on a march myself against Hellas, and am taking my sons and my brothers and my relations and friends, dost thou dare to make any mention of a son of thine, seeing that thou art my slave, who ought to have been accompanying me thyself with thy whole household and thy wife as well? Now therefore be assured of this, that the passionate spirit of man dwells within the ears; and when it has heard good things, it fills the body with delight, but when it has heard the opposite things to this, it swells up with anger. As then thou canst not boast of having surpassed the king in conferring benefits formerly, when thou didst to us good deeds and madest offer to do more of the same kind, so now that thou hast turned to shamelessness, thou shalt receive not thy desert but less than thou deservest: for thy gifts of hospitality shall rescue from death thyself and the four others of thy sons, but thou shalt pay the penalty with the life of the one to whom thou dost cling most." Having answered thus, he forthwith commanded those to whom it was appointed to do these things, to find out the eldest of the sons of Pythios and to cut him in two in the middle; and having cut him in two, to dispose the halves, one on the right hand of the road and the other on the left, and that the army should pass between them by this way.

Chapter 23: At This, My Zygite Bench

23.01: (182–89) The wounded man is Cleton, who had been hit on the street. They put him on the table. Then Latro writes for a while, beginning at the point when Io pointed out the old camp (Chapter 22).

Cleton regains enough strength to tell them that Hypereides was captured and taken to the palace. Prince Thamyris is facing resistance from other lords who wish to put Kotys's son on the throne. He has sent Nessibur and Deloptes to capture Hypereides to strengthen his position.

Acetes will lead a fake Rope Maker group to rescue him. Latro goes on his own. On the street, Elata tries to stop him but fails. Then, near the palace, Io catches up with him. Latro must bring her back to the house and this causes him great turmoil. He goes out again, by a less direct way.

Chapter 24: The Boar

24.01: (189–90) The great creature is inside, after Latro enters the palace, after Latro climbs the wall, after Seven Lions saves him.

24.02: (190-97) To back up: Latro goes to the palace, creates a diversion, climbs over the wall, enters a door. He equips himself with shield, helmet, and javelins. Thamyris invites him into the great hall. Thamyris believes Latro is Pleistorus, and talks about Thracian ambition to conquer the world.

Thamyris tells Latro to kill Hypereides.
Latro identifies the musky aroma as being that of a boar.
Myth: In Greek mythology, Thamyris was a Thracian singer.
Herodotus: When Thamyris says of the Thracians, "None but the Indians are more numerous—none but the Rope Makers more warlike. Were we united—as we shall be—no nation on earth could resist us!" (195) he echoes Herodotus:

> Now the Thracian race is the most numerous, except the Indians, in all the world: and if it should come to be ruled over by one man, or to agree together in one, it would be irresistible in fight and the strongest by far of all nations, in my opinion. (Book V, 3)

This proves to be nearly prophetic when Alexander the Great (356–323 BC) of nearby Macedonia rises to power about a hundred years later.

Chapter 25: Farewell to Thrace

25.01: (197–200) In the palace, melee erupts. Latro cuts the boar and it rips into the Thracians.

Things look dire, but then the door opens to a pack of hounds. To avoid them, the boar charges outside.

With Oeobazus and much gold, the party leaves Thrace.

Latro is writing on the ship, composing chapters 23 through 25.

Heracles: The hero's fourth labor was with the Erymanthian Boar.

25.02: (200–201) Latro learns that in Thracian art a boar called Zalmoxis is the foe of Pleistorus, the war god.

Herodotus: Things get complicated with this "boar called Zalmoxis" detail. Herodotus tells of a Thracian god Salmoxis (Book IV), but he is a holy man of immortality who does not seem connected with boars:

> 95. This Salmoxis I hear from the Hellenes who dwell about the Hellespont and the Pontus, was a man, and he became a slave in Samos, and was in fact a slave of Pythagoras the son of Mnesarchos. Then having become free he gained great wealth, and afterwards returned to his own land: and as the Thracians both live hardly and are rather simple-minded, this Salmoxis, being acquainted with the Ionian way of living and with manners more cultivated than the Thracians were used to see, since he had associated with Hellenes (and not only that but with Pythagoras, not the least able philosopher of the Hellenes), prepared a banqueting-hall, where he received and feasted the chief men of the tribe and instructed them meanwhile that neither he himself nor his guests nor their descendants in succession after them would die; but that they would come to a place where they would live for ever and have all things good. While he was doing that which has been mentioned and was saying these things, he was making for himself meanwhile a chamber under the ground; and when his chamber was finished, he disappeared from among the Thracians and went down into the underground chamber, where he continued to live for three years: and they grieved for his loss and mourned for him as dead. Then in the fourth year he appeared to the Thracians, and in this way the things which Salmoxis said became credible to them.

> 96. Thus they say that he did; but as to this matter and the chamber under ground, I neither disbelieve it nor do I very strongly believe, but I think that this Salmoxis lived many years before Pythagoras. However, whether there ever lived a man Salmoxis, or whether he is simply a native deity of the Getai, let us bid farewell to him now.

The historian tells of a man who brought Pythagorean thought to Thrace, and founded a cult promising a pleasant afterlife to followers.

Myth: Boars in Thrace are connected with the Thracian Rider, as his prey. Boars in Greece are connected with the War God, Ares, as his symbol.

25.03: (201–202) Latro asks Hegesistratus about the hounds. The elder admits he did not see them, he only heard them, but they are Cynthia's.

Hegesistratus and nymph Elata go for a swim.

25.04: (202–205) At the island Sign-of-Thrace they rest. Hypereides tells the locals about the battle in the palace, and how they helped restore the throne to Kotys, son of Kotys, from the would-be usurper Thamyris. Hypereides compares it to Fennel Field.

One woman wonders if the boar was really Zalmoxis, but Hypereides dismisses the idea.

Geography: Sign-of-Thrace is Samothrace.

Onomastics: Zalmoxis is a "shape-changing shaman deified; his name is presumably derived from the Thracian word *zalmo*, 'skin'" (*Arete* glossary).

Commentary: Wolfe also called Orpheus a shaman in the glossary.

Herodotus: Returning to the topic of Zalmoxis, the historian gives a curious detail about an important rite of his followers (Book IV):

> 94. And their belief in immortality is of this kind, that is to say, they hold that they do not die, but that he

who is killed goes to Salmoxis, a divinity, whom some of them call Gebeleizis; and at intervals of four years they send one of themselves, whomsoever the lot may select, as a messenger to Salmoxis, charging him with such requests as they have to make on each occasion; and they send him thus:—certain of them who are appointed for this have three javelins, and others meanwhile take hold on both sides of him who is being sent to Salmoxis, both by his hands and his feet, and first they swing him up, then throw him into the air so as to fall upon the spearpoints: and if when he is pierced through he is killed, they think that the god is favourable to them; but if he is not killed, they find fault with the messenger himself, calling him a worthless man, and then having found fault with him they send another: and they give him the charge beforehand, while he is yet alive. These same Thracians also shoot arrows up towards the sky when thunder and lightning come, and use threats to the god, not believing that there exists any other god except their own.

The killing of a messenger to the god seems shamanistic, similar to the Ainu practice of killing tame bears to take messages to the gods.

End of Part 2

Synopsis of Part 2: The Apsinthinan Labor (Chapter 9 to 25)

Latro's group crosses the Melas, entering the territory of the Apsinthii, and Latro sees a big rider with a hunting lion. They make common cause with a group of Amazons. Latro is attracted to Pharetra, a wounded Amazon, perhaps in part because her hair color is close to his.

At the town Cobrys they meet resistance from the palace. There are two temples, one for the War God and the other for the Mother of the Gods. Latro tries to kill sleeping Hegesistratus, but it was a trap. Hegesistratus tells how he lost his foot through the treachery of the rival family.

Tensions with the palace escalate. Latro's group retreats into a sacred cave and Latro meets Cybele, mother of the gods.

She gives him a task, to steal the horses of the sun. He does this. The boy Polos joins the group.

The Amazon Pharetra is killed.

Letro has a mounted duel with King Kotys, but the king flees and is killed by his own.

The new king Thamyris captures Hypereides. To rescue him, Latro sneaks into the palace. Thamyris seems possessed, and tries to get Latro to kill Hypereides. Latro sees a large boar behind the throne. There is a climactic battle where the boar kills Thracians and celestial hounds arrive to chase it out of the hall.

Latro's party sails away. At an island they learn more about Thracian mythology, and there is a hint that the weirdness was a battle between local gods.

Part 3

Chapter 26: In Cimon's Garden

26.01: (209–16) Themistocles, Cimon, and Xanthippos meet with Latro, Oeobazus, Hypereides, and Hegesistratus. They talk about Oeobazus's death in Thrace as the official story and the Mede adopts the new name of "Zihrun." They plan how Zihrun will go back to the Empire.

Themistocles, Cimon, and Hypereides are Athenians and from both factions. They support Zihrun. They describe their factions. They support Latro, too.

Pronunciation: "Cimon" is pronounced *Keé*-mone (*Arete* glossary).

Herodotus: The historian describes the escape and death of Oeobazus (Book IX):

> 118. Those however who were within the walls had now come to the greatest misery, so that they boiled down the girths of their beds and used them for food; and when they no longer had even these, then the Persians and with them Artaÿctes and Oiobazos ran away and departed in the night, climbing down by the back part of the wall, where the place was left most unguarded by the enemy; and when day came, the men of the Chersonese signified to the Athenians from the towers concerning that which had happened, and opened the gates to them. So the greater number of them went in pursuit, and the rest occupied the city.

> 119. Now Oiobazos, as he was escaping into Thrace, was caught by the Apsinthian Thracians and sacrificed to their native god Pleistoros with their rites, and the rest who were with him they slaughtered in another manner.

Wolfe maintains this as the "official story."

Chapter 27: Io Weeps

27.01: (216–20) Latro's legal status is slave of Pausanias, because when the Rope Makers took him from Kalleos, she applied to Pausanias for compensation and got it. To counter Pausanias's claim, Hypereides re-establishes his own, stating that he never received full payment from Kalleos.

So the plan is for Latro to go to Rope, where Pausanias will free him and declare him a resident of Rope, a "Neighbor."

Hegesistratus and Elata are to leave the group.

Spartan Terms: As the footnote says, "Neighbor" here is *perioikos*.

27.02: (220–23) Latro learns further details, that the poet Pindaros is also trying to free Latro by claiming Latro was serving Hill when captured.

Cimon gives Latro a letter for Cyklos the judge in Rope.

They are at a farm of Cimon's.

Chapter 28: Mnemosyne

28.01: (223–30) The dinner party introduces a young Pericles and his tutor Damon. Afterward, Simonides takes Latro aside to perform sacrifice to the Lady of Memory. Then he instructs Latro on building a memory palace. Latro is distracted at first by a giant woman whose face is wracked with grief.

The palace seems to be located in the desert south of the Mediterranean, with a river to the west. In making this palace, Latro meets the winged lion woman who is also the Earth goddess.

Simonides: His poetry appeared in *Mist* (Chapter XXXVII, 283). In addition, this famous poet really did invent a system of mnemonics.

Commentary: Latro's memory palace looks like the Precinct of Amun-Re at Egyptian Thebes. From the river, a corridor of sphinxes leads toward the gigantic structure.

Chapter 29: The Palace Walls

29.01: (231–32) The next morning Hegesistratus, Elata, and Zihrun set out. Then little Io has a talk with Latro about Thrace: When they were in the cave there, Latro had heard a dog outside, and Hegesistratus went out and the Thracians did not stop him (see Chapter 8, 142). She mentions this now because she heard the dogs the previous night.

There is now a taller boy in addition to Polos.

29.02: (232) The Median boy rides in the cart. Also with them are slaves Diallos and Tillon.

Commentary: The Median boy is Artembares.

29.03: (232–37) Latro writes more about the winged lion woman at his memory palace. He answers her riddle, saying it is a traveler, who rides a horse until he loses it, then walks for a time until he uses a staff.

She mentions Swollenfoot, then she begins to give him a tour of the palace. But after a bit of conversation, she flies up to the palace top and stays there.

Inside the palace, Latro sees a statue of the dancer he had just seen at the party, but when he touches it, the statue shatters.

In the morning the dancer, Anysia, tells him she dreamed of dancing for him, but then he pushed her and she died.

Myth: "Swollenfoot" is Oedipus, who answered the riddle of the Sphinx in his famous way.

29.04: (238) Latro finds he can recall the memory palace better than the house in which he was born.

Chapter 30: Tower Hill

30.01: (238–40) Latro's group is visiting Adeimantus, the man who had commanded the Tower Hill ships at the Battle of Peace. He has spoils from many Riverland ships.

The party-goers will all visit the theater.

Geography: Tower Hill is Corinth; Riverland is Egypt.

Commentary: Little Io had spoken before about her experience at theater.

30.02: (240–46) Pasicrates the Rope Maker, now the man with one hand, visits. Io warns Latro that they fought in the Troad, where Latro cut off his hand.

Pasicrates says he forgives Latro, and mentions that regent Pausanias wants Latro to participate in the Pythic Games at Dolphins, held every four years for the Destroyer.

The ghost of the Median boy appears to warn Latro obscurely about angry soldiers from Kemet at the house.

Latro talks to Io and Polos about sword fighting. Io claims to have killed her man in Thrace.

Chapter 31: From the Tomb

31.01: (246–51) At dawn, Latro writes of the night before: the party goes to the theater. Afterward Latro and Seven Lions visit wine shops. At the third or fourth, Seven Lions finds a Babylonian girl who can speak one of his languages. They go off for a tryst.

Things get very strange for Latro. He feels drunk, then like a wave has crashed over the city.

He finds himself in a vast cavern. He comes upon an old man and asks him his name. The man admits he was Gortys when alive. They see Sisyphus rolling his stone. Latro helps Sisyphus and moves the stone to the hilltop, where it splits.

Latro finds himself in a deep hole in the street. Seven Lions helps him out, and Latro brings Sisyphus along.

Myth: Gortys, son of Stymphalus, was the founder of the town Gortys in Arcadia. Sisyphus, the founder of Corinth, was given his famous punishment by the gods for his self-aggrandizing craftiness and deceitfulness.

Heracles: The great hero rescued Prometheus at one point, which seems similar to this exploit.

31.02: (252–53) Jumping ahead, the girl, named Bittusilma, marries Seven Lions (also known as "Hepta Leones") and they plan to leave the group soon, thereafter divorcing near Babylon.

Latro talks with Sisyphus. Sisyphus says Latro must be the help sent to him by the river god Asopus, as they are related.

At the house of Adeimantus they find the soldiers from

Riverland terrorizing everyone.

Onomastics: Bittusilma means "house of perfection" (*Arete* glossary).

Myth: Regarding Sisyphus and Asopus, the river god asked Sisyphus the identity of his daughter's rapist. Sisyphus offered to tell, only if he would receive a fresh water spring in Acrocorinth. Asopus gave him the spring; Sisyphus told him the rapist was Zeus; Zeus began trying to work revenge upon Sisyphus.

Chapter 32: For the Second Meal

32.01: (254–60) Latro's party, on the road to Rope, has stopped for the second meal (evening) at the lake where Heracles killed so many Stymphalian birds. Latro asks if Pasicrates had been disturbed by ghosts the night before, as little Io had. All the ghosts went away when exorcised by the magus who had fallen into the forgotten tomb with Latro.

There had been earth tremors all over Tower Hill that night. A great stone rolled into the sacred spring at the summit of the Acrocorinth and split. Pasicrates reads this omen.

Io later tells Latro her suspicion that Pasicrates has a ghost hand, since Latro's sword cut it off.

Heracles: Direct and pointed allusion to the sixth labor of Heracles, the episode of the Stymphalian birds.

32.02: (260–61) Pasicrates borrows Polos for a trip to town. Upon return, Polos trembles and will not speak. Latro confronts Pasicrates and promises to kill him, even in the marketplace of Rope, if he hurts Polos.

32.03: (261) Latro reads his scroll by moonlight. He weeps about Pharetra.

Chapter 33: Bull Killer

33.01: (261–62) Latro launches into a confusing bit. A mysterious goat man referred to Polos as "Kain-Tauros." Apparently taking this as meaning "bull killer," Latro now fears the boy.

Little Io gives Latro information, including an itinerary of their recent past together: Thrace, Thought, and Tower Hill. She says she does not remember her family.

33.02: (262–69) Latro believes he neglected to write for at least a day. Now he is at a house in Bearland.

They set out but the road is blocked by a landslip. They find a ditcher to be their hired guide. His name is Aglaus. Aglaus asks Io about each member of the group.

Latro seems to have a memory of Eutaktos: "I remembered the sacrifice of the girl, and how Eutaktos had encouraged his men until he died" (266). This is about the meeting with Ge.

They arrange to stay with Ortygenes, whose son Lykaon had just been killed by a boar. Then the hunt is on. Latro rides a bay colt he comes across.

Latro casts the killing shot.

Then later he sees Polos as a boy-horse.

Myth: Latro mentions Fortuna (268), a Roman god.

Latro Memories: "[T]his day, my childhood, and the fight at the temple" (266). This suggests that he can always remember the fight at the temple, but this contradicts previous text.

Wolf: The name "Lykaon" is tied to another werewolf story. Lykaon was a king of Arcadia who served the flesh of his son to Zeus, who turned him into a wolf.

Commentary: So the "kain-tauros" is not "bull killer" but "man-horse." Polos is a centaur.

Chapter 34: The Feast Is Over

34.01: (270–73) Looking over his scroll, Latro wonders what he meant by "goat man."

The day is spent on funeral rites for Lykaon.

34.02: (273–75) Aglaus talks with Latro about the letters being pictures. Aglaus thinks the goat man is a certain god who lives in the mountains of Bearland. His name is All. Io says this god aided the men of Thought at the battle of Fennel Field.

The mourning father Ortygenes asks Latro if he is a Budini, or of a tribe of the Getae. He says his line fought at Iion. He speaks some poetry: "'Some marks of honor on my son bestow...'" He says he is a king in hiding, a king of the Achaeans.

Myth: So the mysterious "goat man" was Pan, it seems.

Onomastics: "Ortygenes" is an ancient Greek name. To my eye it looks like "A Quail is Born."

Geography: Fennel Field is Marathon.

Homer: The poetry is from Book I of the *Iliad,* a scene where the goddess-mother of Achilles pleads for him to Zeus.

Getae: "Barbarians of the northern forests; the Budini are a tribe belonging to this group" (*Arete* glossary).

Herodotus: The historian writes about the Getae (as "Getai") and the Budini (as "Budinoi") in Book IV. Locating the Getae on the Lower Danube, in what is now Bulgaria and Romania, he declares the Getae believe in Zalmoxis. (Initially "Getae" and "Goth" were distinct, but over several centuries, historians came to see "Getae" as synonymous with "Goth" in being the original source of German tribes.)

As for the Budini, Herodutus locates this tribe in Russia on the Don River (the Tanaïs):

> 21. After one has crossed the river Tanaïs the country is no longer Scythia, but the first of the divisions belongs to the Sauromatai, who beginning at the corner of the Maiotian lake occupy land extending towards the North Wind fifteen days' journey, and wholly bare of trees both cultivated and wild. Above these, holding the next division of land, dwell the Budinoi, who occupy a land wholly overgrown with forest consisting of all kinds of trees.(Book IV, 21)

According to the historian, the Budini is the tribe the Neurians settled among: "The Neuroi ... left their own land and settled among the Budinoi" (Book IV, 105).

In addition to the mixture of Budini and Neurians there is a third group, the Hellenic Gelonians. The Gelonians built the city that was later razed by Darius the Great:

> 108. The Budinoi are a very great and numerous race, and

are all very blue-eyed and fair of skin: and in their land is built a city of wood, the name of which is Gelonos, and each side of the wall is thirty furlongs in length and lofty at the same time, all being of wood; and the houses are of wood also and the temples; for there are in it temples of Hellenic gods furnished after Hellenic fashion with sacred images and altars and cells, all of wood; and they keep festivals every other year to Dionysos and celebrate the rites of Bacchus: for the Gelonians are originally Hellenes, and they removed from the trading stations on the coast and settled among the Budinoi; and they use partly the Scythian language and partly the Hellenic. The Budinoi however do not use the same language as the Gelonians, nor is their manner of living the same.

Commentary: "Nations are like men—growing old, never young" (275). This observation also matches what the text shows of gods, where Ge for the slaves of the Rope Makers is so old, yet she speaks of other places where she is young; and in Thrace where the "still forming" nature of the Thracian rider is merging with Pleistorus, fighting against a Zalmoxis merging with the boar.

34.03: (275–76) In the morning they enter the Silent Country. Themistocles gives Aglaus money and dismisses him, but he follows anyway. Latro and Seven Lions hire him.

Having Aglaus near makes Latro recall a silver chariot. It is not in the memory palace, it is among rocks.

Commentary: Aglaus is a memory booster for Latro, perhaps the reason he remembered the fight at the temple in the previous chapter. Here he is recalling the silver chariot Cybele had him stand in, but he cannot remember any of the context.

34.04: (276) Latro asks Pasicrates about the Achaeans. Pasicrates says they were destroyed by the Dorians, his own tribe.

Achaeans: "An ancient tribe, displaced by the Dorians" (*Arete* glossary). This "Dorian displacement" matches what had been said by the Slaves of the Rope Makers in *Mist*, chapter XXXI.

Commentary: This model seems to be one of successive invasions. First there were the Gaea-worshipping farmers, presumably Pelasgians; then came the Achaeans, who merged their gods and goddesses with those of the Pelasgians; then the Dorians came to displace the Achaeans and violently suppress the Gaea-worship of the farmers.

Chapter 35: Cyklos of Rope

35.01: (277–82) Pasicrates runs ahead to Rope and Latro's group is met outside the city by all five judges. They meet Queen Gorgo and her son King Pleistarchos, a boy.
    Latro's group is staying with Cyklos the judge.
    The next day will be a full moon. The ceremony will begin at the rising of the full moon. The event will honor the Triple Goddess. A Rope Maker sponsor will accompany each special person, about two thousand, who will be freed and made a resident of Rope. Latro's sponsor is Hippoxleas.
    Latro goes through his memory palace process to remember all the points.

35.02: (282) Seven Lions shows Latro a jail cell where a friend had been held (Hegesistratus, but Latro does not remember).

35.03: (282–85) Cyklos talks with Latro privately, mainly about the games, and while he admits that Rope has lost a lot of prestige after Peace, Clay, Mycale, and Sestos, he contends that they will soon sweep Athenian Themistocles from the board.

Chapter 36: Bloodstained

36.01: (285–91) At the palace of prince Pausanias, Latro reads the artifacts to see how King Leonidas died. Perhaps from touching this, Latro's fingers become smeared with fresh blood.
    Pausanias shows a letter about his shipment of spoils, entrusted to one Muslak, who has paid a surety of 800 darics.
    Commentary: Latro does not remember, but he fought directly with Leonides (*Mist* chapter XXXVII). Here he examines the clothing and rules out the killing weapon as arrow, sword,

dagger, lance or spear. From the previous text it seems to have been a thrown shield (*Mist*, 282).

Later, Latro tells Polos that the killing blow for king Leonides had come from a soldier standing above the downed king, the thrust from a javelin. So perhaps Latro's thrown shield knocked the king down, and another soldier finished him off with a held javelin.

36.02: (291–92) Little Io says there is something about Latro's servant Aglaus that reminds her of (nymph) Elata.

Chapter 37: The Dead Man's Stare

37.01: (292–30) Queen Gorgo, the boy king, and a driver arrive in the chariot. Latro races and wins.

The moon rises and the ceremony begins. Pausanias give Themistocles the silver chariot that Latro had seen before.

When the night grows thin, murder breaks out, as freed slaves are slaughtered.

The Silver Chariot: Previously introduced as Cybele's vehicle, this item suddenly becomes complicated with other associations. Herodotus mentions that the Spartans gave Themistocles a gift of the best chariot in the region (VIII, 124), so Wolfe matches that aspect; but Herodotus does not say it was silver or somehow divine. The historian reports that Xerxes had a "sacred chariot" of Ahuramazda, an important symbol of his empire. It was pulled by white horses, and no one rode in it, the handler walking beside it, as it was for the god alone (VII, 40). Herodotus writes that it went across the famous bridge of boats, with Xerxes following in his own chariot (VII, 55).

So there are three chariots: the silver chariot of Cybele; the Spartan gift chariot; and the Persian sacred chariot.

Wolfe might be hinting that the Spartan gift chariot is the Persian sacred chariot. Herodotus states that Xerxes left the sacred chariot on the Thracian Chersonesus for safe keeping, but when he tried to pick it up on his later retreat, it had been lost (VIII, 115). Wolfe's Pausanias might be giving away a choice but gaudy and impractical piece of war booty.

Thucydides: In his book *The History of the Peloponnesian War*, a conflict that ran from 431 to 404 BC, the historian describes an infamous "ceremony of the helots" which seems similar to the event Latro was a part of. First Thucydides sets the context of why helot manpower was needed:

> The attacks of the Athenians upon Peloponnese, and in particular upon Laconia, might, it was hoped, be diverted most effectually by annoying them in return, and by sending an army to their allies, especially as they were willing to maintain it and asked for it to aid them in revolting. The Lacedaemonians were also glad to have an excuse for sending some of the Helots out of the country, for fear that the present aspect of affairs and the occupation of Pylos might encourage them to move. Indeed fear of their numbers and obstinacy even persuaded the Lacedaemonians to the action which I shall now relate, their policy at all times having been governed by the necessity of taking precautions against them. The Helots were invited by a proclamation to pick out those of their number who claimed to have most distinguished themselves against the enemy, in order that they might receive their freedom; the object being to test them, as it was thought that the first to claim their freedom would be the most high-spirited and the most apt to rebel. As many as two thousand were selected accordingly, who crowned themselves and went round the temples, rejoicing in their new freedom. The Spartans, however, soon afterwards did away with them, and no one ever knew how each of them perished. (IV, 80, 1–4)

Commentary: In a text with werewolves preying upon the living and the dead, it seems significant that this Spartan horror is committed under the full moon. We have seen nasty work by crescent-moon Huntress and new-moon Hecate, but this atrocity is for full moon Selene.

End Part 3

Synopsis of Part 3: From Thought to Rope (Chapter 26 to 37)

In Thought Latro says goodbye to Oeobazus (now "Zihrun"), learns the technique of a memory palace, and answers the riddle of the winged lion woman.

At Tower Hill he meets one-handed Pasicrates again, then helps King Sisyphus complete his task.

On the road to Rope they join a boar hunt and Latro sees Polos as a boy-horse.

The ceremony at Rope is a thing of great beauty and monstrous treachery.

Part 4

Chapter 38: The Pythia

38.01: (303) Latro at Dolphins. Little Io tells Kichesippos that she has been intimate with Latro, but Latro knows she is lying.
Geography: Dolphins is Delphi.

38.02: (303–304) Io and Kichesippos urge Latro to write. He seems depressed. The prince, Cyklos the judge, Seven Lions and his wife, Pasicrates, Polos, Aglaus, and Amyklos are there.

38.03: (304–10) They visit the young pythoness for a cure to Latro's condition. Latro hears the python. The girl says one thing, the priest says another.
She, in the voice of Pausanias, says, *"Thou art royal, royal be."*
The priest says,

Not gems nor spears can forge a crown,
what gods raise up, men drag down.
Though queens in rags, they queens remain.
Gracious in aid, their favors gain.

Afterwards Polos gets Latro to ride an old horse. Up on the mountain the horses stop at a temple to Artemis. A woman greets him. It is Elata. Polos, Aglaus, and old Amyklos are there.
Elata is there to represent the Triple Goddess. Amyklos, Polos, and Aglaus are there for her foe, Gaea. (Aglaus was directed by little Io to go with Elata on this occasion.) Then Sisyphus arrives as a friend of Latro's.
Myth: Python is "Gaea's sacred serpent, slain by the Destroyer; it haunts the oracle he wrested from her" (*Arete* glossary). This alludes to the Achaean invasion of Helles.
Mystery: So many queens, but who are the queens in rags? One is Ge, as seen in *Mist* (Chapter XXX, 229).

38.04: (310) Kichesippos is a slave of the prince. Some Crimson Men are slaves now, and they will be sold with their rich goods when more have come to watch the Pythic Games.

Chapter 39: Diokles

39.01: (311–14) Diokles is the gymnastes training Latro for the games: boxing, pankration, and chariot race. Diokles is also training Pasicrates for races. Pasicrates told Diokles that little Io is Latro's but they share Polos. Diokles insists that they avoid such intimacies until after the games.

Satyricon: This ancient Roman novel has the two main characters sharing and arguing over the beautiful slave boy, so Pasicrates makes it sound as though he and Latro are in a similar arrangement with Polos.

39.02: (314) Little Io tries to seduce Latro, with herself or Elata, but the attempt fails.

Satyricon: The notoriously naughty novel has various women trying to cure the hero's impotence through seduction, and failing.

Commentary: This detail is probably what caused *Soldier of Arete* to be banned in Canada.

39.03: (314–16) Diokles trying to learn what is wrong with Latro. Tells him the story of Heracles and the cart, where the famous hero tells the farmer to do it himself.

Latro speaks to Diokles about his feelings, how "Man is a wolf to men."

Commentary: Latro seems to be making the equation between Spartans and werewolves.

39.04: (316–18) Latro takes a long solitary walk. After a while he is accompanied by a ghost. It is Sisyphus. He tells Latro that the king and queen of the dead dislike Sisyphus because of how he got away before.

Sisyphus tells Latro that while they want to kill Pasicrates, they will not because it would not help Latro. Instead they will force him to "let go."

Later Latro is visited by a woman. She is the dancer Anysia, first met in Chapter 28 (225), now hired by Diokles. She eases

Latro's melancholy.

Chapter 40: For the Sake of Days Past

40.01: (318–20) Little Io admits she had agreed to Elata's attempt to try and cheer Latro before.

Reading his scroll about Pharetra gives Latro joy, and he wonders if she died of her wound.

40.02: (320–23) The mantis Tisamenus talks with Latro. Trioditis (the Triple Goddess) said, "The queen must win, and thus the queen must lose." Tisamenus believes the winning queen must be Queen Gorgo, so Latro must win the chariot race.

Tisamenus says that Pasicrates wants to marry so he can adopt Polos.

Tisamenus tells about his cousin Hegesistratus. He admits he was the informant who called down the Rope Makers upon Hegesistratus, leading to his imprisonment. He says he fears Latro's sadness is due to a charm by his cousin, and he asks Latro to point him out.

40.03: (323–25) Latro goes to enter the rolls. As a test, he is asked to quote some poetry. The official gives an example: "'For thee, my son, I wept my life away . . .'"

A goddess helps Latro: "You golden lyre, Apollo's and the muses' . . ."

And Pindaros finds them with a joyful reunion.

Homer: "'For thee, my son . . .'" is from *The Odyssey* (Book XI), where the ghost of Odysseus's mother laments the grief that he gave her in life.

Pindaros: "You golden lyre . . ." is the opening of Pindar's "First Pythian Ode" (470 BC).

Chapter 41: The God Himself Shall Rule

41.01: (326–31) The Pythic Games involve competitions of music and singing as well as the athletics.

Themistocles of Thought arrives in a silver chariot.

It turns out that Bittusilma of Babylon had been freed in the same way Latro and Seven Lions had been.

The Amazons show up, five women. One kisses him, and she is Pharetra.

The judges are against allowing Amazons to compete. Themistocles works around the problem, and the Amazons will use his silver chariot if they compete.

Latro still seems a bit suicidal.

41.02: (331–35) In the evening, Latro and Io visit Pindar at his inn. The poet sings, and Latro dreams: A faun leads him to a temple where Polos and Amyklos are both half-horses, and there is a woman.

Tisamenus and Pasicrates come. Things get complicated.

The woman tells Pasicrates to take back his hand.

Pasicrates strikes Aglaus. Amyklos knocks Pasicrates down and holds him down. Polos talks to Pasicrates of love. Pasicrates reaches to Latro and his hand is restored.

The song ends and Latro wakes up.

Walking back to their inn, Latro and Io meet Hegesistratus with the Amazon queen and Pharetra. They all go to see the horses.

Pharetra goes to the inn with Latro and Io. There is a woman in Latro's bed, but the women fight and the Amazon wins. Later Pharetra tells him that her queen will kill her if she loses the race to Latro.

41.03: (335) Latro watches the sun rise. "I have not forgotten the night that crushed me."

Chapter 42: Pausanias Rages

42.01: (336–37) Pausanias is furious because all of his loot from the Battle of Clay was entrusted to a Crimson Men ship; they had been promised a safe passage by Tower Hill, but they were pirated by a ship from Hundred Eyed, which took it to Cyparissa, the port nearby.

Latro speaks to the Crimson Men held under guard at the agora. Their captain Muslak knows him from before, and calls him "Lewqys." Muslak swears he will return Latro home to Luhitu if Latro frees him, his crew, and his ship.

Onomastics: Muslak is an Aramaic name that might mean "foundling."

Commentary: The earlier talk of Hypereides using piracy upon Crimson Men (Chapter 8) seems to have been played out on this ship, despite war heroism and promises of safe passage.

42.02: (337–38) Pausanias watches Latro practice and discusses Polos riding in the contest for boys.

42.03: (338–39) In Aglaus's dream, Latro knocked him down, then helped him up. Latro asked him if he was sure.

Pasicrates later tells Latro in private that in his dream he struck Agalus, then Latro gave him his hand back.

Tisamenus takes Latro to be seen by Orsippos of Hundred-Eyed, who doubles the bet on the race.

42.04: (339–40) First day of the Pythic Games. Latro tells Aglaus to give him a daily reminder and update about the slaves in the market.

42.05: (440–41) That night, Latro spends time with Pharetra. He talks her into buying weapons for him. The other woman shows up and screams at Pharetra until the Amazon chases her off.

42.06: (341) The day of the most popular foot race. Latro practices wrestling.

42.07: (341) Pasicrates is beaten for failing to win a footrace. The prince sends him to Tower Hill.

42.08: (341–44) The day of the five trials. Anysia meets Latro and tells him she is his true love and the Amazon he calls Pharetra is a cruel fake because the real one died in Thrace. The fake is Hippostizein. This was cooked up by Io to save him. Anysia learned all this from Elata.

42.09: (344) Latro's plan involves driving a chariot to the ship.

42.10: (345) Latro wins wrestling. He signs a deed giving the children to Pindaros.

Chapter 43: Pindaros of Thebes

43.01: (345–48) The poet writes this chapter, dedicating it to the Shining God.

He describes the chariot race. The Amazon is in the lead. Latro passes, but then shoots off the track and away.

The Amazon wins for Athens. The prize is given to Themistocles, who gives it to the Amazon Queen Hippephode, who donates the container to Apollo, which forges peace between Theseus's foes (Amazons) and Theseus's city (Athens).

But war has come to the sacred city. Latro has attacked.

Hegesistratus confesses his bribery and strategy have failed, and he will die the death he foresaw in Thrace.

Latro's scrolls will be placed in the urn given to the temple.

Commentary: Pindaros seems genuinely hurt by Latro's actions.

The Silver Chariot: The fact that the gift chariot is being pulled by milky-white horses of the Sun is a strong match for the sacred chariot of the Persians. If it is not the same chariot, it is at least a clear imitation of it.

Strangely enough, having an Amazon drive the vehicle validates the theory of Ahuramazda being the War God in disguise (*Arete,* Chapter 22), since it looks like the sacred chariot is being driven by a devotee of Ares, and she is disguised as another Amazon.

Mystery: Hegesistratus "sat grieving his lost wife" (347) might be a misunderstanding by Pindaros, or perhaps Elata is missing.

Herodotus: The death of Hegesistratus is mentioned in Book IX:

> 37. So he at that time having thus escaped them took refuge at Tegea, which then was not friendly with the Lacedemonians; and when he was healed and had pro-

cured for himself a wooden foot, he became an open enemy of the Lacedemonians. However in the end the enmity into which he had fallen with the Lacedemonians was not to his advantage; for he was caught by them while practising divination in Zakynthos, and was put to death.

End of Part 4

Summary of Part 4: From the Oracle to the Games (Chapter 38 to 43)

Latro is depressed and the oracle at Dolphins speaks riddles, but then up on the mountain Latro has a meeting with representatives of earth goddess, moon goddess, and himself (38). Latro begins training for the games (39). He is reunited with the poet Pindaros (40) and then the Amazon Pharetra (41).

Latro has a dream that others seem to have had, too, but there are little differences. Anysia the dancer tells Latro that Pharetra is fake. He continues working on his secret plan (42).

At the race, Latro drives off the track. He goes down to the port, frees the Crimson Men, and sails away with them in their ship (43).

APPENDICES FOR SOLDIER OF ARETE

Appendix L2-1: Historian Notes

Because *Soldier of the Mist* ends at Sestos, there seemed a hint that Thucydides would prove foundational to the second Latro novel, since Herodotus ends his History at Sestos and Thucydides begins his History at Sestos. Instead, Wolfe jumps another generation and honors Xenophon, whose *Hellenica* is a continuation of the *History of the Peloponnesian War* by Thucydides.

Xenophon is celebrated in *Soldier of Arete* with a dedication and an epigraph. Perhaps it is for his experience as a Greek mercenary of the Persian Empire and a writer of the same in his *Anabasis*. While he was in a later generation than Latro, Xenophon's situation of being a mercenary on the losing side is similar.

As in *Soldier of the Mist,* Herodotus has a large impact on Latro's narrative, but this time the text cuts both ways. Readers previously familiar with Herodotus know that Oeobazus was a human sacrifice in Thrace, so this causes a tension through the first half of the novel. Even when Oeobazus suddenly walks up and thanks Latro in Chapter 21, this comes after the ghost of Raskos, and the ghost of Artembares, so that it seems very likely that Oeobazus is also a ghost.

Arete shows Wolfe's creative use of details from Herodotus. Marc Aramini's massive Wolfe-tome *Beyond Time and Memory* (2020) notes that there are two figures named "Oeobazus" in *The Histories* of Herodotus: one being the designer of the pontoon bridge, and the other having three adult sons murdered by the Persian king of kings. Aramini points out that Wolfe combined these two into one as an example of Wolfe's detailed reading of Herodotus, but I will focus on the impossibility: the Oeobazus who lost three sons (Book IV, 84) saw them murdered by Darius prior to the Scythian campaign (513 BC), which was 33 years before the pontoon bridge was built. Then the historian writes that the pontoon bridge had already been built at that time, designed by a Samian named Mandrocles (IV, 87). The Imperial army crosses this bridge and attacks the Scythians, so clearly the pontoon bridge in question is an earlier construction. Wolfe moves the Oeobazus of three sons (IV, 84) to the timeframe of Pythios (VII, 38) so that Xerxes is the murderous monarch; and there is no talk of an earlier pontoon bridge.

Aside from the ancient historians, another text emerges in *Arete,* thereby revealing a heretofore hidden influencer in *Zalmoxis: The Vanishing God* (1970) by Mircea Eliade. This book is a collection of eight scholarly essays, two of which have a direct bearing upon the Latro novels.

One is "Zalmoxis," an examination of the enigmatic figure first mentioned by Herodotus. Eliade argues that Zalmoxis was a shaman, of the same type as Orpheus and others, providing a basis for Wolfe's similar statements. Describing the training process, Eliade writes, "[S]hamanic initiation includes dividing the body into fragments, renewal of the organs and viscera, and ritual death followed by resurrection, experienced by the future shaman as a descent to the Underworld" (41). Eliade notes that "During [the shaman's] ecstatic journeys he is able to change into a wild beast and in that form to fight with other shamans" (41).

The other essay, "The Dacians and Wolves," is about wolf names for families, tribes, and nations radiating outward from the Indo-European birthplace of the Eurasian steppe. Footnote 22 mentions "the myth of the she-wolf with twins, and its roots in the archaic beliefs of the pastoral peoples of the Asian steppe" (4).

Appendix L2-2: The Latro Of Arete

Even though Latro was revealed to be a Roman at the end of *Mist,* in *Soldier of Arete* his deeper roots of hidden heritage begin to emerge in notes on Scythians, Getae, and Budini.

In Thrace, when Latro meets the Amazons from Scythia, he falls in love with one who has reddish hair that is nearly like his own.

On the road to Rope, when the old Achaean prince in hiding asks Latro if he is of the Getae or the Budini, this is the second time we have been exposed to Budini, because Kalleos, the madam of the Athenian brothel, had told him she was sold as a child slave from the Budini, and she has red hair and blue eyes. She thinks she was stolen as a little girl (*Mist,* 102).

If Kalleos is in her thirties in 479 BC, then she was born 520 to 510 BC. Was there anything noteworthy in Scythia in that era?

It seems that there was. King Darius of Persia invaded European Scythia in 513 BC. He grew frustrated chasing the nomads around, but he did burn a city. I will let Herodotus tell it (Book IV):

> 121. Having formed this plan the Scythians went to meet the army of Dareios, sending off the best of their horsemen before them as scouts; but all the wagons in which their children and their women lived they sent on, and with them all their cattle (leaving only so much as was sufficient to supply them with food), and charged them that they should proceed continually towards the North Wind. These, I say, were being carried on before:

> 122, but when the scouts who went in front of the Scythians discovered the Persians distant about three days' march from Ister, then the Scythians having discovered them continued to pitch their camp one day's march in front, destroying utterly that which grew from the ground: and when the Persians saw that the horsemen

of the Scythians had made their appearance, they came after them following in their track, while the Scythians continually moved on. After this, since they had directed their march towards the first of the divisions, the Persians continued to pursue towards the East and the river Tanaïs; and when the Scythians crossed over the river Tanaïs, the Persians crossed over after them and continued still to pursue, until they had passed quite through the land of the Sauromatai and had come to that of the Budinoi.

123. Now so long as the Persians were passing through Scythia and the land of the Sauromatai, they had nothing to destroy, seeing that the land was bare, but when they invaded the land of the Budinoi, then they fell in with the wooden wall, which had been deserted by the Budinoi and left wholly unoccupied, and this they destroyed by fire. Having done so they continued to follow on further in the tracks of the enemy, until they had passed through the whole of this land and had arrived at the desert. This desert region is occupied by no men, and it lies above the land of the Budinoi, extending for a seven days' journey; and above this desert dwell the Thyssagetai, and four large rivers flow from them through the land of the Maiotians and run into that which is called the Maiotian lake, their names being as follows,—Lycos, Oaros, Tanaïs, Syrgis.

In other words, Darius razed a "wooden wall" that may have been just a wall, but it was probably Gelonos, the single city of the Budinoi, a settlement boasting a wall "thirty furlongs in length and lofty ... all being of wood" (IV, 108). Whether wall or city, it had been evacuated in advance, rather like the Russians abandoning Moscow to Napoleon. All the refugees went somewhere.

Recall the griffin statuette that Latro seemed to recognize in the tent of Pausanias, regent of Rope. Remember the chain of quotes from Herodotus that implied the griffin was a war trophy from the household of Xerxes himself. Apply this to Herodotus writing about the Scythian campaign of Darius, father of Xerxes, and it seems possible that the griffin was obtained by Darius around the time that the Budinoi city was burned.

Gene Wolfe was very interested in onomastics. Regarding his name, in 1984 he wrote, "My own means a Wolf is Born. If you know me . . . you won't be able to see the barbarian armies streaming toward Rome when you read that, but they are there" (*Plan[e]t Engineering,* xvi). That is, he paints the picture of late Imperial Rome falling to invading Germanic tribes.

Yet clearly Wolfe sensed a discontinuity to that image, since Rome was founded with the help of a she-wolf, which requires that a wolf cult was already there before the city was. So in the Latro novels he examines the wolf cults in the ancient world. The city of Gelonos, with its combination of Hellene, fair-skined Budini, and wolf-cursed Neuri; a city destroyed by Darius the Great; seems too good to ignore.

Latro's Powers And Demeter's Curse

Latro's strange memory problem seems to be the result of Demeter's curse upon him at the Battle of Clay, but Latro also has a number of powers:

- Spirit Sight: ability to see the dead, see monsters, see gods.
- Spirit Reveal: ability to make spirits visible through touch.
- Temporary Resurrection: Thygater, possibly Pharetra.
- Nike Stands Behind Latro: (*Mist,* Ch. XXVII; *Arete,* Ch. 10).

The first three powers share a certain necromantic quality. Perhaps they were given by Demeter, since she is all about life.

Nike is a different category. Nike is associated with Zeus and Athena. It also seems unlikely that Demeter would grant this to Latro, even if she could. So the default position is that Zeus or Athena gave it to Latro, which, in the initial context, implies that Latro encountered Zeus or Athena at the same time he met Demeter, yet there is no textual support for this supposition.

A major mystery of the Latro novels is what happened to Latro near the temple at the battle. Jeremy Crampton spells it out in "Some Greek Themes in Gene Wolfe's Latro novels," beginning with, "Demeter/Gaea has taken away his memory because of an as yet unidentified offence." A paragraph later, he pushes further:

> Latro at least may have gone into the temple. Kore the Maiden remarks that he is no longer as stubborn as he was with her mother (*Mist,* p. 120) which seems to hint that he at least talked with Demeter, and perhaps insulted her. It is interesting to speculate that perhaps his comments had something to do with memory or forgetting, which gives his punishment a kind of divine justice.

Crampton hints at hubris, and we can bolster this by noting Latro later threatened the Maiden with his bare hands, so the idea that he might have raised his sword against Demeter seems likely.

In order to establish the shape of the encounter, let us establish the context.

Latro is born into and raised within a wolf cult, so he belongs to Demeter, at least during the childhood he can remember.

As a youth he becomes a soldier, presumably turning to worship Mars (who has some clear differences from Ares). Latro joins the army of Xerxes, so there is a possibility that he begins worshipping Ahura Mazda. The Persian army crushes everything in its path, with highlights at Thermopylae and the razing of Athens. The Battle of Plataea is minor, since the next target is Corinth, and after that, Sparta.

This is the moment when Latro meets Demeter. She curses him, and the war abruptly ends.

This strongly suggests that the stunning success of the Persian army was due to Latro having Nike. That is, Latro had been given Nike before.

Demeter's curse removed all of Latro's allegiances, leaving him a victory-promised hero without a cause.

She also changed him from being a tool of men into being a tool of the gods.

Whether or not Latro worshipped Ahura Mazda, he definitely served this god by fighting in the Persian army. Ahura Mazda had a certain "solar" quality, being a god of light, and this might be the poetic justice of Latro's memory only being a solar day in duration.

Appendix L2-3: Timelines

At Sestos, see prisoners (chapter 1) 1 day
Executions; buy cloaks; meet Hegesistratus (chapters 2–4) 1 day
Set out in ship for Pactye; meet nymph (ch. 5–6) 1 day
At Pactye (chapters 7–8) 1 day

<Break. Gap mentioned in foreword, being one week or more.>

Thrace
On the road: Morning nymphs; evening Amazons (ch.9) 1 day
At Cobys: Through the town and camping, (ch. 10–11) 1 day
Latro's day under guard (chapters 12–15) 1 day
Meet goddess; steal horses (chapters 16–17) 1 day
Dawn attack by peltists; exchange and duel (ch. 18–19) 1 day
Raskos before dawn; village (chapters 20–21) 1 day
At dawn find farm; reunion; back to town (ch. 21–25) 1 day
Preparing/sailing/Sign-of-Thrace (chapter 25) 3 days

<Second break mentioned in foreword, between Samothrace and Piraeus (port of Athens).>

From Thought to Rope
Thought (chapters 26–28) 1 day
road (chapter 29) 1 day
Tower Hill (chapter 30) 1 day
road, end at lake (chapters 31–32) 1 day
<break>
Bearland boar hunt (chapter 33) 1 day
Bearland funeral, walk through Silent country (ch. 34) 2 days
Rope arrival (chapter 35) 1 day
Rope ceremony (chapters 36–37) 1 day

\<break: third gap mentioned in foreword.\>

The Pythic Games
At Dolphins (chapter 38) 3 days?
Training (chapter 39) 1 day
Training (chapters 40–41) 1 day
 "Four days until boxing" (chapter 42.03) 1 day
First Day of Games (chapter 42.04) 1 day
Foot race (chapter 42.06) 1 day
Five trials; Latro has meal with Anysia (chapter 42.08) 1 day
Wrestling? Boxing (chapter 42.10) 1 day
All-power fighting (chapter 42.10) 1 day
Last Day: Chariot race (chapter 43) 1 day

Appendix L2-4: Ben Hur Throws The Race

At the climactic chariot race, Latro goes straight at the curve and leaves the track. The silver chariot, driven by the fake Pharetra, easily wins for Athens and the Amazons.

But the celebration is cut short by word that Latro has brought war to the port.

Hegesistratus confesses to Pindaros that the silver chariot was too heavy; that love of the Amazon for Latro would weaken her, not him; and that despite all this stacking of the deck, Hegesistratus has failed the goddess of his enemies (the Huntress) and thus he will die the death he had already foreseen.

Pindaros notes that, paradoxically, Prince Pausanias has gained ten times what he lost.

Pindaros reports the sighting of Latro on the ship as it sailed away, how there stood at his side a slender woman with a bow, undoubtedly the Huntress.

It is hard to say what happened,exactly, yet it appears that Latro won.

The complexities of the race began much earlier in the complexities of the Thracian adventure.

"Thrace"
Teams
- Get Oeobazus Team—Hypereiades
- Kill Oeobazus Team—King Kotys (acting on Orphic verse)
- Buy Sacred Horses Team—Queen Hippephode (sent by War God)
- Oust King Kotys Team—Thamyris (possessed by Zalmoxis)

Three-way Contest
- War God—mentioned in Orphic verse
- The Huntress—mentioned in Orphic verse; served by Elata and Hegesistratus
- The Sun—mentioned in Orphic verse

Two-way Contests
- Earth goddess versus Moon goddess—Cybele helps Latro and Amazons steal horses, presumably against Bendis (the Huntress)
- Game between Athena and Artemis—Athena angling for payback regarding the murder of Kekrops by a serpent woman in *Soldier of the Mist*
- The Thracian Rider versus the Boar—the Rider wants to kill the Boar; the Boar wants to take direct control of Cotys palace from the indirect control by the Huntress

Other Players
- Fake Rope Makers—Acetes
- Orpheus—a singing shaman killed by followers of Dionysus
- Zalmoxis—a shape-changing shaman; probably the Boar, in whole or in part.

The Huntress spells out both the Thrace job and the race job in talking to Latro, Elata, and Hegesistratus (43–44), saying
- They will soon meet a queen (Hippephode) with a strong protector (Pleistorus) whom the Huntress plans to use to flush a boar (Zalmoxis)
- They are to help her (Hippephode) until the moment she must lose
- My queen, the prince, and this queen (Hippephode)
- Latro must drive for my prince

What remains unclear is the identity of the "my queen" and "my prince." The best guess might be Queen Gorgo and Prince Pausanias, both of Rope (Sparta), which the Huntress owns.

◆ ◆ ◆

Thrace goes like this.
- King Kotys has been spooked by a prophecy.
- He tries to prove it wrong by killing Latro.
- His successor, Zalmoxis, tries to prove it wrong by bend-

ing Latro.

The case of the phantom boar is a curious one.

Perhaps it starts back in *Mist:* When the statue of Demeter moves its hand from resting on the boar's head in order to point at the floor, it seems a boar spirit is freed (Latro feels that the air is "filled with soft yet heavy noises, as if some massive beast stirred and stamped where it could not be seen"). Then in *Arete* when Latro is tumbling with the nymph and the Huntress appears, the goddess had been hunting something. After the Huntress leaves, little Io senses something big moving around—perhaps the phantom boar. In this light, it seems as though the boar spirit released by the statue of Demeter attached itself to Latro, using him in a passive way as a vehicle, until disembarking on the Thracian Chersonese.

At the palace, the boar is clearly invading and influencing, a case of spiritual warfare. The Huntress seems to have had her way in flushing the boar, which implies that the War God was using Latro as a vehicle.

Following this logic, if the boar came from Demeter, did she want Zalmoxis to win? That might be the case, if it means that Bendis (the Huntress) would lose the palace.

Since the Huntress "won," she gets a victory point. If the earth team won at the end of *Mist* with the wolf sacrifice, then at this stage the earth team and the moon team are tied.

Still obscure is the game between Athena and Huntress. Is it because of Athens versus Sparta? Is it because on the beach (*Mist,* Chapter XI) the serpent woman killed Kekrops, whose name marks him as belonging to Athena?

"The Race"
The Teams
- Pausanias (Sparta)—driver Latro
- Themistocles (Athens)—driver fake Pharetra in the silver chariot given by Rope

The Queens
- Amazon Queen Hippephode

- The Maiden, Queen of the Dead
- Spartan Queen Gorgo
- Queen in rags (Hippephode, Gaea, little Io)

Players
- Crimson Men—hired by Pausanias; pirated by Hundred-Eyed
- Little Io—agent of Latro, she allows Elata to try and help Latro, then allows fake Pharetra
- Hegesistratus and Elata—agents of the Huntress
- Anysia the dancer—agent of Diokles, but she came from Thought (with Themistocles?)
- Fake Pharetra—put up to it by Hegesistratus (he confesses) or Io (Anysia says)
- Amyklos, Polos, Aglaus—agents of Gaea
- Sisyphus—agent of Latro
- Pindaros—agent of Latro

The conclusion of the chariot race has many winners in different ways.
- Athena (Athens) wins over Artemis (Sparta)
- Pausanias wins by acting regal and letting Latro escape
- Latro wins what Artemis had promised him
- Artemis rides with Latro on the ship, despite all the contradictions

If Artemis has won another point against the earth team, then that is two out of three, and she wins the bout.

The puzzle remains as to how Latro's action can be considered a win for Artemis. It might be as simple as removing Latro's Nike from the field.

L2-5: Apollo Prophecy Checklist (Number 2)

At the Temple of Apollo (*Mist,* Chapter III), the god says to Latro, "Only the solitary may see the gods. For the rest, every god is the Unknown God" (11). After a bit of conversation, Apollo says:

> A. "I prophesy that though you will wander far in search of your home, you will not find it until you are farthest from it.
>
> B. Once only, you will sing as men sang in the Age of Gold to the playing of the gods.
>
> C. Long after, you will find what you seek in the dead city.
>
> D. "Though healing is mine, I cannot heal you, nor would I if I could; by the shrine of the Great Mother you fell, to a shrine of hers you must return.
>
> E. Then she will point the way, and in the end the wolf's tooth will return to her who sent it
>
> F. Look beneath the sun...." (11–12).

The version of the pythoness goes this way:
    1. Look under the sun, if you would see!
    2. Sing! Make sacrifice to me!
    3. But you must cross the narrow sea.
    4. The wolf that howls has wrought you woe!
    5. To that dog's mistress you must go!
    6. Her hearth burns in the room below.
    7. I send you to the God Unseen!
    8. Whose temple lies in Death's terrene!
    9. There you shall learn why He's not seen.
    10. Sing then, and make the hills resound!
    11. King, nymph, and priest shall gather round!
    12. Wolf, faun, and nymph, spellbound. (15)

The Apollo and Pythoness lines seem related at points:

A/Pythoness
A
B/2, 10–11
C
D/5
E/6
F/1

More of the lines seem fulfilled:

A (Chapter fulfilled in Mist)
A
B (V: king of Nysa, nymph Hilaeira, priest Pindaros)
C
D (XIX: meet the Maiden)
E (XIX: meet the Maiden)
F

P (Chapter fulfilled in Arete)
3 (7: cross narrow sea)
12 (41: wolf Latro, faun Aglaus, and nymph Elata)
1 (32: Cybele says, Look under the sun)

L2-6: Latro And The Gods (2)

A list of supernatural details.

- The portent of the fish (ch. 1)
- Activates Elata (ch. 5)
- Meet the Huntress (ch. 6)
- The ghost boy (ch. 8)
- The Thracian Rider (ch. 9)
- Meet Cybele (ch. 16)
- Raskos (ch. 20)
- The ghost boy again (ch. 21)
- The Boar (ch. 24)
- Meet Mnemosyne (ch. 28)
- Meet Sisyphus (ch. 31)
- Casting out ghosts (ch. 32)
- Meet Pan (ch. 33)
- Old blood flows (ch. 36)
- Sisyphus again (ch. 38)
- The Dream (Ch. 41)

SOLDIER OF SIDON

Soldier Of Sidon

Edition cited: Tor (hb), ISBN 31664-1, November 2006, 319 pp.

Dedication: "To Sir Richard Burton"
   Commentary: Sir Richard was not only an adventurer who explored the headlands of the Nile, he was also a translator of *The Book of the Thousand Nights and a Night* (1885).

Epigraph:

> The AEthiopians were clothed in the skins of leopards and lions, and had long bows made of the stem of the palm-leaf, not less than four cubits in length. On these they laid short arrows made of reed, and armed at the tip, not with iron, but with a piece of stone, sharpened to a point, of the kind used in engraving seals. They carried likewise spears, the head of which was the sharpened horn of an antelope; and in addition they had knotted clubs. When they went into battle they painted their bodies, half with chalk and half with vermilion.
>
> —Herodotus

Commentary: This quote comes from the soldier lists of Herodotus we have become so familiar with (Book VII, 69). It appears to be the Rawlinson 1860 translation.

Foreword: (13–20) How Gene Wolfe received a new translating task of a scroll found in the lake of the Aswan Dams, a body of water covering the ancient nation of Nubia. Written in archaic Latin.

   Notes on Ancient Egypt
- Gods
- Beer taverns
- Polygamy
- "Singing girls"
- Slavery
- Invasions and in-fighting

- "Sea Peoples" 1176 BC
- Geography
- Army
- Climate change (drying of Sahara) over 20,000 years
- Relations with Nubia

Part I

1. Ra'Hotep Says

1.01: (23–30) Ra'hotep tells Latro to write on this scroll, and to read it every morning.

Latro is in the city Sais of Kemet, with Ra'hotep, Muslak, and Myt-ser'eu. Muslak tells Latro this is where Latro wanted to go. Latro admits he could not remember his own name, and Muslak says his memory comes and goes, but now it is gone. Alarmed, he takes Latro to a healer.

Muslak explains to the healer that he returned Latro to his home in Luhitu, but the next time he visited, Latro's wife asked Muslak to take Latro to Riverland to find out what had happened to him. This wife was left behind.

Muslak tells of his first meeting with Latro. It was at a location upriver. Latro had a hundred men and was trying to get hired for the Great King's army. The task was to march to Byblos, Muslak's city near Sidon.

The second healer, Ra'hotep, admits he was the healer who had treated Latro at Clay, and at that time Latro was called one of Sidon's soldiers.

The group is summoned to Prince Achaemenes at the White Wall.

Latro naps the afternoon away.

Onomasatics: Ra'hotep is Egyptian for "Ra is Satisfied." Achaemenes is the Greek version of the Persian name *Hakhdmanish,* meaning "Friend" (*Sidon* glossary).

Myth: Set is a complicated god of ancient Egypt. He is a god of magic. He is the god of the red colored land of the far south. He is involved in the conflict between Osiris (lord of the dead and rebirth) and Isis (a goddess of magic).

Hathor is a love goddess. Herodotus equates her with Aphrodite.

Ra is a sun god.

Gene Wolfe had written before about the Set/Typhon connection in an article on names in **The Book of the New Sun,** and he gave this curious detail: "Real Egyptians call this wicked brother Set or Seth . . . He had white skin and red hair, both of which they were prejudiced against" (*Castle of Days,* 254).

Geography: Sais was an Egyptian town on the Nile delta. Byblos was at this time one of the four Phoenician vassal kingdoms established by the Persians, the others being Sidon, Tyre, and Arwad. But note that Byblos is not Sidon; marching from Egypt, Latro would presumably reach Sidon before Byblos.

Dionysus: Herodotus wrote that the grave of Osiris (Dionysus) was located in Sais (Book II, 171).

Commentary: The novel begins with what seems to be a betrayal by Muslak, in that they are in Sais rather than Rome. After that is resolved, Muslak outlines the action Latro took previously, marching from a location up the river toward Byblos, which explains why he is called a soldier of Sidon. The mystery of Latro's previous time in Egypt seems solved.

2. In the Evening

2.01: (31–36) Latro and Muslak go to Hathor's temple. Latro sees the goddess. She makes a deal with him.

Muslak pays one daric for Neht-nefret, a singing girl, to be his river wife.

The singing girl who approaches Latro is the one the goddess had mentioned to him, so Latro selects her. Another daric for Myt-ser'eu.

Onomastics: Neht-nefret, the "nefret" part means beautiful; "Tall Sycamore" (*Sidon* glossary).

History: In the Foreword, Wolfe writes about two examples of Theban tomb art showing "singing girls" (16), one with girls dancing naked, which seems to be from the Tomb of Nebamun, and the other a naked girl with her musical instrument, probably from the Three Musicians in the Tomb of Nakht.

Herodotus: This renting/marriage of river wives sounds a bit like the historian's description of the Babylonian marriage market in Book I, a curiosity covered before in the notes to "The Woman Who Went Out" (*Mist,* 15.01).

3. In the Shade of the Sail

3.01: (37–38) Latro is writing with ink and a reed. Muslak sells all the hides, which takes most of the morning. They are in the delta on the river Pre.

3.02: (38) Never drink the river water.

3.03: (39–40) Myt-ser'eu says the Great King treated her people terribly in her mother's time.
   Timestamp: This probably refers to the Egyptian rebellion which Xerxes personally suppressed in 484 BC. After this event, it took Xerxes four years to build his army up again, at which point he launched the second invasion of Greece. So this is the timeframe when Latro came to Riverland before, yet Myt-ser'eu does not say it was when she was born, she says it was in her mother's time.

3.04: (40) They pass white temples as massive as mountains.
   Geography: The first pyramids encountered when heading up the river are at Giza.

3.05: (40–42) Much later, at an inn, with music and dancing. Latro drinks Egyptian beer with clay straws, a detail mentioned in the Foreword.
   Latro writes on the roof of an inn. He wants to visit Sidon to find more of his past. Muslak says he will help.

4. Night Has Gone

4.01: (43–44) More than one day later, while in a ship at anchor, Latro sees the boat of a god bring the sun. The god has the head of a falcon, and he is accompanied by a baboon, and a woman with a plume in her hair.
   Myth: The sun god Ra was said to travel through the sky on a boat, in contrast to the chariot of the sun among the Hellenes. Riding along is falcon-headed Horus, with the baboon of Thoth, and the goddess with a feather is Maat. Horus was a sky god, an avenger against Seth. Thoth was a scribe of the gods. Maat was a

goddess of truth, justice, and wisdom.

4.02: (44–45) Latro has headlice from the inn, so the women shave his head. Myt-ser'eu makes him a headcloth.

Commentary: If Latro's hair is reddish, shaving his head would also help his appearance in a culture that is prejudiced against red hair.

4.03: (45) Latro and Muslak practice the foreign language.

4.04: (45–46) Three warships pass them. They pass the city On, heading for Mennufer.

Geography: "On" is a Hebrew name for Heliopolis (now a northeastern suburb of Cairo); "Mennufer" is Memphis, at the mouth of the Nile Delta (now 20 km/12 miles south of Giza).

4.05: (46–47) At Mennufer, Muslak hurries to the White Wall while Latro and his river wife visit shops and dine at an inn. They sleep at the inn.

Herodotus: The historian writes that the Persians have the "White Fortress" at Memphis (Book III, 91). (Other sources state that an early name for the city was "The White Walls" or "Fortress of the White Walls.")

4.06: (47–48) The next day's shopping is interrupted by a summons to White Wall. Latro goes off exploring the fortress and gets lost. Back with his waiting friends, they meet the priest Thotmaktef.

Latro holds back from writing more about him.

4.07: (49) Latro's notes on the White Wall itself.

5. Sahuset Summons Us

5.01: (51–58) The satrap, Prince Achaemenes, recalls that a "Latro" fought three warriors at Artaÿctes's order.

The job he has for them is far south, past Wast, past Nubia, into Nysa. There are cataracts on the river. The ship must be carried around each after the first.

Qanju, a man of Parsa, will go with them accompanied by

three soldiers. Sahuset, a man of Kemet, will go with them. Captain Muslak asks for five additional soldiers.

Qanju will be the leader. He is of the Magi tribe.

Latro declares that if he finds his footsteps from years before, he will follow them.

Qanju agrees and sets Latro in charge of the soldiers.

Qanju points out they are seven: Qanju, Muslak, Thotmaktef (in charge of Sahuset, "the most difficult post of all"), Latro (in charge of the soldiers), Azibaal (first mate), and the river wives Neht-nefret and Myt-ser'eu.

They are back at the inn, briefly. Sahuset sends a woman to summon them to him. Latro notes that when he first saw Thotmektef, the priest was accompanied by a phantom baboon.

History: Achaemenes, brother of Xerxes, was satrap of Egypt from 486 to 459 BC. Interestingly, during the second Persian invasion of Hellas he had led the Persian-allied Egyptian fleet and had survived the Battle of Salamis (480 BC) which Latro refers to as the Battle of Peace.

Qanju was the name of a governor of Cambyses in the Egyptian city Koptos.

Geography: "Wast" is Waset (Thebes of Egypt), in modern Luxor, 800 km/500 mi south of the Mediterranean. Nubia here is the last region of civilization on the upper river, with Nysa as the legendary land beyond.

Geography: There is talk of the Tin Isles as a distant place. Herodotus mentions this location (Book III, 115) but admits he does not know where they are, beyond a sense it is on the other side of Europe. They remain a mystery. "*Tin Isles.* The Scillys and the Cornish coast" (*Sidon* glossary).

Onomastics: Azibaal means "my strength is the god Baal."

Myth: "Seven Gods in a Boat" is a Japanese trope. The Takarabune "treasure ship" is piloted through the heavens by the Seven Lucky Gods during the first three days of the New Year. The seven gods are: Ebisu (fisherman), Daikokuten (demon hunter), Bishamonten (warrior), Benzaiten (beautiful woman), Jurojin (elder), Hotei (drinking), and Fukurokujo (resurrectionist) or Kichijoten (happy woman).

6. I Remembered

6.01: (59–66) Latro and Myt-ser'eu sleep until nightfall, then go to meet Sahuset. They follow Sahuset's servant Sabra across the city.

Sahuset hopes to help Latro remember. He speaks of divinity as infection. He is a priest of the Red God. The Red God commands the evil xu. He is the desert god. He is Set.

In exchange, Sahuset asks Latro to give him any scroll or inscribed stone he might find in the south. When Latro agrees to this, his host tells him to put down a carving of a winged fish he had picked up. Sahuset takes a few drops of blood from Latro's finger that had touched the carving, and puts this blood into a vial. He takes a drop of blood from Myt-ser'eu and gives it to Sabra, who rubs it on her cheeks.

To help Latro, Sahuset will give him an indwelling xu to fight the curse. He will stay there until he is expelled.

While waiting, Latro tries to talk with Sabra but finds her a wax image.

The summoned xu is like a man with a mask of fresh leaves.

When Latro's memory comes, it comes fast. Latro remembers his wife Justa, and his father, mother, and sister. But then the xu is gone.

Latro rushes to write.

Myth: Set's animals are horse, hippopotamus, pig, and crocodile. The winged fish statue is probably Abtu, a fish that flies ahead of the solar boat at sunrise.

Bible: Sahuset says, "The ignorant masses believe the Red God evil because he commands the evil xu. If he tells an evil xu to leave a man, that xu must go. They are compelled to obey him in all things" (61). This sounds like the response Jesus gave to the Pharisees:

> But when the Pharisees heard it, they said, This fellow doth not cast out devils, but by Beelzebub the prince of

the devils.
And Jesus knew their thoughts, and said unto them, Every kingdom divided against itself is brought to desolation; and every city or house divided against itself shall not stand:
And if Satan cast out Satan, he is divided against himself; how shall then his kingdom stand?
And if I by Beelzebub cast out devils, by whom do your children cast *them* out? therefore they shall be your judges.
But if I cast out devils by the Spirit of God, then the kingdom of God is come unto you.
Or else how can one enter into a strong man's house, and spoil his goods, except he first bind the strong man? and then he will spoil his house. (Matthew 12:24-29)

Onomastics: "Justa" is a Latin name meaning "fair." Thotmaktef is listed as a name in *Ancient Egyptian Names for Dogs* (1996), and my guess is that "Thot" is for his god Thoth. Sahuset might be "sahu" (spiritual body) plus Set, his god.

Commentary: Sabra is a wax figure who comes to life. She seems to be like a golem of wax rather than clay.

7. Thotmaktef

7.01: (67-68) Thotmaktef suggests the group take on a Nubian, as he would know the country.

7.02: (68-69) Latro disciplines his eight soldiers, three of Parsa and five of Kemet. One is Uro.
Onomastics: Egyptian "Uro" means "King."

7.03: (69) The ship's name is *Gades*. The full population is two women and twenty-seven men.
Onomastics: "Gades" is the Phoenician city Cadiz (in Spain), meaning "holy place" or "holy base."

7.04: (70) There is talk about river horses. Another soldier is Amamu.
Onomastics: Amamu is a name from ancient Egypt. It is on a

coffin at the British museum. It dates from 3721–3503 BC.

7.05: (70–71) Azibaal says there is a third woman onboard. Myt-ser'eu asks who her protector is, but the sailor will not say.

7.06: (71) Latro will stay onboard the ship at night to see about this third woman.

7.07: (71–75) Another soldier is Aahmes.

In the night the third woman comes up from the hold. She knows Latro's name. Then he gets distracted by a cat the size of a dog, a creature that subsequently disappears. Latro can see the woman walking to the village.

There is a quarter moon (72).

Qanju and Thotmaktef come back to the ship to study stars. Latro tells them about the woman. They urge him to write it down.

Onomastics: Aahmes, "leader of the soldiers aboard the *Gades*" (*Sidon* glossary), whose name means "The Moon is Born," or "born of Lah (moon god)." This was the name of the pharaoh who founded the first dynasty of the New Kingdom of Egypt.

Commentary: Based on Latro's history of seeing the ship spirit Europa (in *Mist* chapter XI), it seems likely this third woman is a similar ship spirit. Except for the important fact that others have seen her.

8. Shade

8.01: (77–78) Latro enjoys beauty while sitting near the temple of Sesostris. There is a mountain of white stone.

History: "*Sesostris*. A pharaoh of the Twelfth Dynasty, better known as Senusret" (*Sidon* glossary). Senusret's pyramid is at el-Lisht, 65 km south of Cairo.

Herodotus: The historian describes Sesostris as an Egyptian king who had left pillars in Asia Minor and Egypt, showing himself as a warrior with equipment from Egypt and Ethiopia (Book II, 106).

8.02: (78–82) Myt-ser'eu makes Latro write about the meeting in the morning: The mystery of the third woman is spooking the sailors. The leaders discuss it, trying to solve it. The big cat seems to be her protector. They will try something at the Mortuary Temple of Sesostris, a short sail up the river.

9. We Lingered Here

9.01: (83–90) Sahuset brings wine to Latro and Myt-ser'eu. He drinks it unmixed and unburdens himself about how he is the outcast of the ship.

He points out that Myt-ser'eu's name means "kitten" and asks Latro about his response should the priests make a lethal connection between Myt-ser'eu and the phantom large cat. Latro says they will leave.

Sahuset talks of taking Latro to his old temple when they reach it.

Myt-ser'eu says she was driven out of her neighborhood in Sais, which marks her.

Latro asks Sahuset for the truth he was too wise to voice at the meeting. It is that the woman is at least as uncanny as the cat; that the cat is not hers; that neither has done harm, but the attempt to rid the ship of them is likely to do great harm.

Sahuset reads Myt-ser'eu's future for her. Then he does the same for Latro, and says he will have death before sunrise.

Egyptian Terms: "Nine Bows" is a term for foreigners. "Egypt's foreign enemies, a traditional phrase" (*Sidon* glossary).

Bible: Sahuset, talking about a xu possessing a person, says, "No one tries to move into a house that is already inhabited." This sounds similar to the Parable of the Empty House, Matthew 12:43–45:

> When the unclean spirit is gone out of a man, he walketh through dry places, seeking rest, and findeth none.
> Then he saith, I will return into my house from whence I came out; and when he is come, he findeth it empty, swept, and garnished.
> Then goeth he, and taketh with himself seven other spirits more wicked than himself, and they enter in and

dwell there: and the last state of that man is worse than the first. Even so shall it be also unto this wicked generation.

10. We Are One

10.01: (91–100) Sesostris arrives and tells Latro to follow. Latro rises, drawing three others with him. All are him. A fifth man is being mourned.

Sesostris labels them Ba, Ka, Shade, and Name. He leads them into the temple. Uraeus is the name of his crown's cobra.

Ammut is there, to eat the unworthy.

They enter the mountain-tomb. The four are judged by 42 gods. Because of his/their confessed sins, they will be attacked by five gods: the faceless god, the god of the Underworld, the Eater of Blood, the Eater of Entrails, and Neb-hrau. But when the gods weigh his heart, they discover he still lives. They send him back. But he has been touched by Osiris, so Sesostris gives him a memory helper in Uraeus.

Latro flies from the temple to the boat, where his five parts reunite.

Onomastics: Uraeus is the term for the sacred crown cobra.

Myth: The 42 gods and the 42 "negative confessions" are based upon the *Papyrus of Ani,* translated by Budge.

11. Uraeus

11.01: (101–103) Uraeus is Latro's slave, a man who vanishes when dismissed.

Latro writes Myt-ser'eu's version of how Latro came to die: After drinking some wine, they slept beneath a tree. She woke to find him dead. She ran to the ship where they were casting out demons. The soldiers carried Latro's body to the ship and Sahuset worked at resurrecting him. Latro returned to life and began to write about his experience.

Little Orphan Annie: Having a henchman who could be called "the faithful asp" provides a link to the comic strip "Little Orphan Annie," where Daddy Warbucks has a problem solver called "The Asp."

11.02: (103) Latro sees a river horse. His soldier Aahmes is from Mennufer.

11.03: (104–10) Latro wrestles with his men. One soldier is Baginu. Latro learns Uraeus has been hunting rats in the hold. The scribe comes down to ask if they have seen the cat or the phantom woman. They discuss how the casting out might not have worked. The time since Latro died seems more than a day: "last night" the scribe saw the cat when they went ashore; not long ago a sailor saw the woman (107). This phantom cat is bigger than before. Uraeus prompts Latro that the scribe's name is Thotmaktef.

Thotmaktef, getting spooked about Uraeus, asks him to lift his head, and then is relieved there is no scar on Uraeus's neck.

After Thotmaktef leaves the hold, Uraeus shows Latro the woman is a wax figure in a coffin-sized box. Uraeus says that he and Latro might force the warlock to make it speak.

Mystery: What is the neck-scarred creature that Thotmaktef was thinking of?

12. I Was Afraid

12.01: (111–17) The warlock in question is Sahuset. Uraeus says the wax woman is Sabra. Sabra wakes up and talks with Latro. Uraeus asks if her master animated her now. She admits he would be angry to learn she was up. Uraeus asks who animated her, but she ignores the question.

Sabra says Sahuset risked Latro's life to make himself great by giving Latro a drug that often causes death.

Sabra asks Latro for blood from either of the singing girls. He refuses. Sabra warns she can be a terrible foe.

Bible: Uraeus speaks to Latro about a "common" trick of a serpent staff that, when anointed with serpent blood and thrown to the ground, becomes a living serpent for a time (112). This echoes the situation of Moses and the Egyptian magicians:

And the Lord spake unto Moses and unto Aaron, saying,

When Pharaoh shall speak unto you, saying, Shew a miracle for you: then thou shalt say unto Aaron, Take thy rod, and cast it before Pharaoh, and it shall become a serpent.

And Moses and Aaron went in unto Pharaoh, and they did so as the Lord had commanded: and Aaron cast down his rod before Pharaoh, and before his servants, and it became a serpent.

Then Pharaoh also called the wise men and the sorcerers: now the magicians of Egypt, they also did in like manner with their enchantments.

For they cast down every man his rod, and they became serpents: but Aaron's rod swallowed up their rods. (Exodus 7:8–11)

Commentary: Sabra, the "wax golem," here reveals a more vampiric side. But she also gives the idea that Sahuset was offering Latro as a sacrifice to Set.

13. The Wolf-Headed God

13.01: (119–20) Ap-uat is the god of soldiers. The soldiers wish to make offerings to this god at his city Asyut. There are complications to this idea.

Myth: Ap-uat is also Wepwawet, which means "opener of the way." He stands in the prow of the solar boat. Now the Boat of Ra is getting so crowded it seems time for another table.

Boat of Ra
God : Realm
Ra : Sun
Horus : Avenger
Thoth : Scribe
Maat : Justice
Ap-uat : Opener
Abtu : Fish

Commentary: The Foreword points out that wolves are

exotic to Egypt, and that the Egyptian wolf-god was "presumably imported at an ancient date from the Near East" (15).

13.02: (120–24) Latro talks with Sahuset. Sahuset offers that he has a woman in a box, but there is an enchantment on the ship that wakes her, which is a happy thing for him. Now it becomes clear that Sabra leaves the ship to visit Sahuset's tent.

Latro says he had a dream of this wolf-headed god, and so he would like to offer sacrifice at the city. Sahuset says this war god was on the pharaoh's standard.

Latro describes the dream. Hearing that Latro said "Girl" as he cut the throat of the wolf, Sahuset admits they must stop at Asyut.

Geography: Asyut was called "wolf-city" Lykopolis. The two most prominent gods were Anubis and Ap-uat.

Commentary: We note that Latro's dream about a wolf with a broken back links to the end of *Soldier of the Mist*. Sabra's role is now a blend of "Dutch wife" sex doll and Pygmalion's statue.

13.03: (125) A warship stops them and Latro feels certain that, due to the delay, they will tie up at Asyut.

14. The Jackal-Headed God Called

14.01: (127–29) The city is filled for the festival.

Latro watches some bullfighting, which is between bulls. The procession is on the river, where images of every city god pass on boats. The image of Ap-uat is a god to Latro.

14.02: (129–34) Tybi is a soldier of Latro. Latro, Myt-ser'eu, and Uraeus set out to meet Anubis in the city of the dead. Latro and Myt-ser'eu get to the place when the sun is low. They have a run-in with grave robbers and loot the bodies. At the inn they hear that a jackal yipped and then urinated on the bodies of three dead grave robbers.

Onomastics: Tybi is the fifth month in the Egyptian calendar.

Myth: The jackal-headed god is Anubis, who is brother to the wolf god.

Commentary: It appears that Latro has done a favor for Anubis.

15. The Scarab

15.01: (135–36) Latro breathes upon the jewelry and the scarab seems to move its wings. It is a sign of Khepri, the eldest god.
Myth: Khepri is the morning sun, the rising sun.

15.02: (136) Latro buys a black lamb and his men drive it to the temple. A strong north wind rises. Captain Muslak believes they will arrive at Wast by nightfall, but Azibaal doubts it.

15.03: (136–41) Qanju talks with Latro about the wolf god. He mentions that the wolf is honored in Latro's city, whose armies march under a wolf standard. The temple has sent a scroll that fell from the rack. This scroll has a prophecy that seems to match Latro as "a hero of Anubis who had forgotten Anubis." The scroll mentions a special shield of Hemuset and where to find it, saying that a scarab will lead him to it. A man will see his entire life reflected in her shield.
Next, Qanju is asking about the third woman.
Myth: Hemuset is the Egyptian goddess of fate and protection. Her headdress bears a shield below two crossed arrows.

16. With Muslak?

16.01: (143–47) Qanju sends Holy Thotmaktef to get river wife Neht-nefret. She arrives with a bandaged hand and tells how she was cut at the inn by a strange woman.
Qanju and Holy Thotmaktef suspect this strange woman is the third woman. They speculate that her cat, a leopard, climbed up, entered the room through the window, and lifted the bar at the door, allowing the woman to enter.
Edgar Allan Poe: The detail of an inexplicable crime secretly involving an animal seems like "The Murders in the Rue Morgue" (1841).

16.02: (147) Latro and Captain Muslak will stay at the same inn and keep watch. Latro's scarab has no wings now.

17. The All-Beast

17.01: (149–54) They are in Wast the Thousand-Gated.

Latro is at watch, and in the night a gong sounds in the corridor. He follows it down the stairs, and then he is trapped by the great cat while a person goes up the stairs.

This time it is Myt-ser'eu who is cut.

Myt-ser'eu mentions her older sister Maftet.

Geography: Waset is Thebes, more commonly known as "Hundred-Gated."

Onomastics: Maftet ("She Who Runs") is a goddess of swift justice.

17.02: (154–56) Qanju hears Latro's report and says that it was the Dark God, Angra Manyu, known by other names among other peoples. Holy Thotmaktef gives six names: Apep, Aaapef, Set, Sut, Sutekh, and Setcheh. Latro asks the healer, who first speaks favorably of the god, and then says the panther serves the Dark God while Sabra serves the healer.

18. The Monkey

18.01: (157–64) Latro, Uraeus, and Holy Thomaktef go to the market to buy wine and water for wounded Myt-ser'eu. Latro admits in writing that he learned about the inn and the panther from reading the scroll.

The wine-seller Agathocles is a Hellene who spoke to Latro the day before, but also seems to almost recall him from the games of years past. Agathocles sells them wine from distant Cimon's estate. For the purest water he leads them to Charthi's house. Charthi tells them his son was lost in the area beyond Yam, where they are going.

Charthi mentions the gold mines of that region. They are legendary. Charthi shows them a map to the gold mines. Beyond Nekhen, beyond Abu.

Agathocles joins the group with a second map showing the exact locations of a dozen mines.

Timestamp: "There was a Latros at the games one year.... He won the pankration, they said" (158).

Onomastics: Agathocles means "good glory," or "Of Good Fame" (*Sidon* glossary). The most famous Agathocles was the tyrant of Syracuse (317–289 BC).

Maps and Legends: There is a real map of the mines that is one of the oldest maps in the world, the Turin Papyrus Map, drawn circa 1150 BC.

Commentary: The reader's fleeting hope that Latro's tasting the wine from Cimon's estate (visited by Latro in *Arete* chapter 26) would open a memory for him is dashed.

Geography: Nekhen, or Hierakonpolis, is a city of Upper Egypt; Abu is Elephantine.

18.02: (164) The monkey talks to Latro, which makes him upset.

Animal Emblem: The baboon is a sign of Thoth and Babi. This monkey seems to be a familiar, presumably like Sahuset's previous "cat" familiar that was exorcised.

Commentary: The monkey says, "So, you did not see Master?" (164). If this refers to Sahuset, was Sahuset invisible? If the familiar is referring to Set, then how did it expect Latro to have seen Set?

19. The Healer's God

19.01: (165–71) Latro practices two-stick fencing with his soldiers. The healer, who has the monkey, tells Latro that the Red One would speak with him on that evening, in the bow of the boat.

To make this appointment, Latro leaves Myt-ser'eu asleep at the inn and goes back to the ship. Sabra appears, then disappears.

Agathocles, who seems to be from Tower Hill, shows up and tells Latro about the strange things back at the inn. How he was visited by a woman, seemingly Myt-ser'eu, and how their activity was interrupted by a knife-wielding woman who slashed the first woman. Then a snake-voiced man grabbed the knife woman, and there was a panther with a man in a dog's head mask. The masked one gestured at the knife woman, who then jumped off the roof.

The healer comes onboard and takes the empty box. They bring the box back and Latro sees inside a battered wax image.

20. Sabra

20.01: (173–74) Latro and Holy Thotmaktef watch Sahuset shaping a woman of wax in the hold. He says it is useful in treating women, as they can point to areas on the figure.

Thotmaktef asks if Sahuset can animate it.

Sahuset seems to deny the ability.

Latro sees the figure blink and look at him.

20.02: (174–77) After sleeping most of the day, Latro forgets. Sahuset says he must wait again for the Red God that night.

Sahuset is from Abu and they hope to get there by night. Beyond Abu is the second cataract.

Herodotus: In Book II the historian claimed to have personally visited Abu (Elephantine):

> 29. From no other person was I able to learn anything about this matter; but for the rest I learnt so much as here follows by the most diligent inquiry; for I went myself as an eye-witness as far as the city of Elephantine and from that point onwards I gathered knowledge by report.

20.03: (177–82) They are at the city Abu. Vayu of Parsa is another of Latro's soldiers, and he calls the city Yeb. Latro and Myt-ser'eu will stay on the ship.

Sahuset tells Latro that Myt-ser'eu was unfaithful to him with Agathocles. He offers to make an amulet to keep her loyal. Latro says she already has an amulet, a bull's head, that Sahuset made for her. The sorcerer says that is for different protection. Then he introduces Sabra as his wife. Uraeus appears and reminds Latro that Sabra is the wax woman. Sabra says that the magicians most often make crocodiles, and she had once been such a wax crocodile.

Sahuset, in rising anger, asks Sabra who animated her that night. She claims it was Latro. Then she turns her charms on Latro, trying to drive a wedge between him and Myt-ser'eu.

Myt-seru'eu enters the scene, followed by another.

Geography: Yeb is another name for Elephantine.

Onomastics: Vayu is an ancient Persian wind god.

Commentary: Sabra's comment on wax crocodiles provides a solid link to "The Magician Ubaaner and the Wax Crocodile" (in Budge's *The Literature of the Ancient Egyptians,* 1914) which tells of a warlock who creates a small wax crocodile that grows large and does tasks for him.

21. Beteshu

21.01: (183–85) The speaking panther tells them Great Seth favors Lucius the Roman and Sahuset of Miam. Lucius and Sahuset are to come to his temple and stay until dawn.

Beteshu the panther reminds Myt-ser'eu that Great Seth saved her. Sabra gives her word that she will leave Myt-ser'eu alone. Sahuset dismisses Beteshu.

Sahuset says he had a familiar that was a cat. Qanju and the priests drove it away, so Sahuset begged Seth to send another. He did and sent Beteshu with it. Beteshu had been a servant of Apep, chief of the bad xu. Seth won him and gave him to Sahuset. Beteshu has eyes of burning gold, no matter his body shape.

Myth: Budge lists Beteshu as a title of Apep.

Geography: Miam (Aniba) in Nubia now flooded by Lake Nasser.

Commentary: So the monkey is the familiar, separate from Beteshu.

21.02: (185–89) Latro, Myt-ser'eu, Captain Muslak, Neht-nefret, and Holy Thotmaktef are at an inn in Abu. Latro writes by early sunlight about the previous: They wait long for the interview with the sagan. The meeting goes well, but they must wait possibly days for a letter and a representative who will join them.

Hearing talk about the Red Land, Latro senses he has been there before.

The landlord of the inn uses a silver lamp shaped like a dove, but later Latro finds it is a common clay lamp. This seems like a godly sign.

Abu is the last civilized town below the first cataract.

Holy Thotmaktef gives harsh advice to the two river wives. Then he says he will find a wife of his own.

Geography: Abu is an island located just downstream of the First Cataract. It marks the division between Lower Egypt and Upper Egypt.

Herodotus: The historian writes that river travel from Sais to Elephantine (Abu) takes 20 days (II, 175).

Commentary: Latro's feeling he had been in the Red Land before sounds unlikely. At Sais it was said he had been further up the river, but this was presumably to Mennufer (Memphis), from which he marched toward Byblos and was hired at Sidon. That being the likely case, his memory of being in the Red Land seems like a false memory or a sign of possible possession.

22. Wise Counsel

22.01: (191–93) Myt-ser'eu tells Latro that Holy Thotmaktef must already have a girl, which is why he spoke that way.

22.02: (193) Latro goes out and asks for the temple of Hathor, where Thotmaktef would get a river wife. He learns there is not one in the city, "None south of Nekhen." Latro goes back to the inn.

Geography: Nekhen is also called Hierakonpolis ("hawk city"). In Upper Egypt, located near Edfu, between Luxor and Aswan.

Commentary: The priest in Sais said that there are seven Hathors along the Great River (33), so Latro is right to check. Sais is one, presumably Nekhen is the last, the likely others include Dendera, Mennufer (Memphis), Heliopolis, Yamu, and Terenuthis.

Mystery: Where did Thotmaktef get his wife?

22.03: (193–97) Myt-ser'eu tells Latro to make Uraeus find a washerwoman. After doing this, Beteshu asks to talk with Latro, reminding him that they both serve Set. Then he calls forth the wax woman, calling her "creature of Sahth," and asks her if she will slay her present husband. Then he warns her he will obliterate her if she kills her present husband.

She returns to her box.

Beteshu says the wax woman woke because Latro is near her. Beteshu says he must not kill his slave the cobra.

Uraeus urges Latro to write.

23. The Water-Path

23.01: (199–203) Holy Thotmaktef brings his new wife Alala, who has a pet baboon.

Kha is the man being sent to the Nubian King. He comes onboard. He says he will ask King Siaspiqa to show Qanju the gold mines. The Hellene will detect the methods of mining used.

Later Latro asks where Alala's pet is, but she is confused by the question, claiming to have no pet.

Latro is sent to find Sahuset in the market and he locates him by recognizing his pet monkey. Aahmes is frightened by this, saying that Sahuset has no pet.

Onomastics: Alala is ancient Greek for the war cry.

Poetry: Pindar wrote of Alala. "Harken! O Alala, daughter of Polemos! Prelude of spears! To whom soldiers are sacrificed for their city's sake in the holy sacrifice of death" (Dithyrambs, Fragment 78).

Myth: Alala is an attendant of Ares, the god of war.

History: Siaspiqa was a Kushite king of Meroë from 487 to 468 BC.

Timestamp: That Siaspiqa is king implies that the current year is before 469 BC. The year 469 BC would be ten years after the Battle of Clay at 479 BC.

23.02: (203) The ship is in the canal around the cataract. Latro vows to walk ahead the next day.

Herodotus: In Book II the historian describes the canal around the cataract:

> 29. From the city of Elephantine as one goes up the river there is country which slopes steeply; so that here one must attach ropes to the vessel on both sides, as one fastens an ox, and so make one's way onward; and if the rope break, the vessel is gone at once, carried away by the violence of the stream. Through this country it is a voyage of about four days in length, and in this part the Nile is winding like the river Maiander, and the distance amounts to twelve *schoines*, which one must traverse in this manner. Then you will come to a level plain, in which the Nile flows round an island named Tachompso.

23.03: (204) The next day Myt-ser'eu reminds Latro, and he goes with Uraeus and two soldiers, Aahmes and Baginu.

23.04: (204–205) Uraeus urges Latro to return to the ship before dark to guard against Myt-ser'eu being unfaithful. They do so, the ship meeting them at mid-afternoon. Qanju asks Latro about the village on the other side of the canal.

Alala tells Latro about spotted deer taller than trees. She talks of Yam and Kush, and of her people the Medjays.

Geography: The Medjays were warriors, so perhaps her war name makes more sense.

Geography: Kush was a kingdom in Nubia. "Yam. The Nile valley between the second and third cataracts, once independent" (*Sidon* glossary).

24. Agathocles

24.01: (207–208) The Hellene returns to the ship. Myt-ser'eu complains to Latro about him.

They are camped by a town of mud brick beside the river. Agathocles talks in private for a long time with Sahuset.

24.02: (208) Latro sees a baboon in front of Sahuset's tent. It is eating a monkey.
Animal Emblem: Baboons are symbols of Thoth, but monkeys are too.
Commentary: Thoth has taken away Sahuset's monkey familiar.

24.03: (208–216) Qanju calls a meeting with Agathocles, Alala, Nehet-nefret, Captain Muslak, healer Sahuset, Kha, and Latro.
Agathocles tells them his search for Kames, son of Charthis, but also of another opportunity for riches involving the mines to the east of the river.
Alala, allowed by Holy Thotmaktef, tells what she knows: that there are places the Nehasyu will not let Medjays graze their cattle. There is a temple at one such place. She was born in Abu, but her people in this area to the east will know.
Agathocles says he went to Miam and spoke to men he knows.
Sahuset objects to the discussion.
Qanju points out the checks and balances involved.
Agathocles gives the news that Kames is being worked as a slave in a gold mine to the east.
Qanju will write letters to the satrap and to the governor at Abu. Azibaal will take them in a small boat to Abu, then catch up.
Qanju asks Alala for advice. She says her people, the Lion People, can be hired to take the mine and free Kames.
Qanju asks Neht-nefret, who offers to infiltrate the place.
Qanju asks Holy Thotmaktef. He thinks Kames is being used as a scribe. He wants to ask among temple scribes.
At Latro's turn, he states they must take Kames by stealth or by force. He suggests Alala take her new husband to meet relatives among the Medjay. Get information from them.
This is the plan. Seven will go.
Geography: Miam in ancient times was an important town of Nubia. Later known as Aniba, today it is flooded by Lake Nas-

ser.

24.04: (216–17) Latro writes on the day they bought horses. Myt-ser'eu argues for Uraeus to join the group, which means another horse. They do this.

25. How Lovely This Is!

25.01: (219–20) After riding a long day, they camp in the Red Land. Latro outlines the group. Holy Thotmaktef is the commander. Latro commands three bowmen: Baginu, Vayu, and Kakia. There is Myt-ser'eu and Alala and the slave Uraeus.

Onomastics: Armenian Kakia, king of Nairi and Habushkia, was defeated by Shalmaneser III of Assyria.

25.02: (220–21) Uraeus finds rock pictures showing men throwing spears at a beast with a long nose and long fangs. At another place Latro scratches his name and a picture of their camp.

A lion roars nearby. Latro sets a watch rotation.

25.03: (221) "We are seven men and two women—no longer as I wrote." But it was six men and two women.

25.04: (221–23) Latro wakes to find his head cradled in the hands of a black man. He talks with him. The sentry comes and says there is nobody there. When Latro shakes hands with the black man, he becomes visible to the sentry. He is Arensnuphis to Latro, the Good Companion to Myt-ser'eu, and Onuris to Holy Thotmaktef. Latro will help him.

Myth: Arensnuphis is a god from the Kingdom of Kush, first mentioned in the third century BC. He is called in Egyptian "the good companion." He is a lion and a human with a crown of feathers and a spear. Onuris is an Egyptian war god who brought his wife Mehit from Nubia; his name means "leads back the distant one."

Commentary: In terms of "divinity as infection" (Chapter 6, 61), Latro just received a heavy load.

25.05: (223–24) Latro travels with Arensnuphis. They halt early. Arensnuphis has Latro read his entire scroll.

They hunt his wife, Mehit, whom he must catch and tame again each year. Latro will see her as a young lioness.

Myth: Mehit is an ancient Egyptian goddess, mainly worshiped at Hierakonpolis and Thinis. In her earliest form she was a reclining lioness with three bent poles sticking out of her back. She is the consort of Onuris, a hunter god worshipped in Thinis.

25.06: (224–25) Latro drives Mehit into the net. When Arensnuphis spears her, she becomes a beautiful black woman. They embrace and disappear, leaving her golden lion skin behind.

26. In the Mine

26.01: (227) Kames brings the scroll and brush and ink, so Latro writes. Myt-ser'eu is nearby, and the man who comes and goes, and Holy Thotmaktef.

26.02: (227–28) Myt-ser'eu visits Latro. She says she has been raped, and she wants to kill the rapists. Latro says he will do that.

26.03: (228) Kames visits to warn Latro. In addition to Kames there is a prince who is a slave.

Latro is in a hut by the smelter. When some guards try to take his scroll, he kills them both. Now he has their daggers.

26.04: (228) The man who got away visits. The captors are looking for the two men Latro killed. Latro is ready.

26.05: (229) There is a noise outside. Kames speaks in two languages. A woman speaks. Someone plays a lute.

26.06: (229) Uraeus and Latro carry away the dead men and hide them. Latro sends Uraeus out to get help.

26.07: (229–30) Uraeus comes back because there are no horses. At night Latro listens to the strange woman talking at the mine. She describes the wax woman. The leader Piy says they will not be lured away so easily, so that Prince Nasakhma might be rescued. He demands that she tell where the box is.

She tells them.

Latro and Uraeus get there first, finding the box and the dead horse that carried it. Now three lie in wait for the men from the mine.

Onomastics: Nasakhma was a Kushite king of Meroë. His reign is not known, but he was the successor of Siaspiqa who reigned 487–468 BC. (King Siaspiqa was mentioned in chapter 23.01.)

Timestamp: If this prince is the same Nasakhma, then it implies that the current year is before 469 BC. The year 469 BC would be ten years after the Battle of Clay at 479 BC.

26.08: (230–31) Leader Piy sends four men with five horses. Latro, Uraeus, and Sabra kill them.

Uraeus urges him to write.

26.09: (231–34) Sabra and Latro go back to the mine. Among the prisoners Latro hands out daggers, one to Nasakhma the prince. (Vayu calls Latro "Centurio.")

Myt-ser'eu plays the lute. Sabra dances, reanimated by Neht-nefret's blood. Sabra has cobras. Unexpectedly, lions aid the fight.

The battle goes quickly.

Later, Myt-ser'eu says Mehit is an Eye of Ra, and a moon goddess.

Myth: The Eye of Ra is a complicated topic, but here it is a pattern wherein a goddess goes forth from Ra and must be brought back to him by another god. Mehit became identified with the "Distant Goddess" myth, along with Hathor-Tefnut.

27. Myt-ser'eu is Gone

27.01: (235–37) Latro and party escape on horses. They are pursued. Latro and his bowmen fight well but are overwhelmed. Latro has a memory of his childhood home. He is taken prisoner and Myt-ser'eu is taken from him.

He writes using his blood.

Latro Memories: "[T]he little house, and the household god squatting by the hearth, ugly and good. My father bringing dried vine dressings to feed our fire, my mother stirring soup."

27.02: (237) The enemies win by holding a knife at Myt-ser'eu's throat.

27.03: (237) Geese fly overhead.

27.04: (238–39) Latro goes over the battle again. The two bowmen and their deaths.

27.05: (239) Latro mentions visions of the fire, a crone, a cow-headed woman, and an eagle on a staff.

Latro writes his last words but cannot find his name.

Commentary: The crone is a childhood memory; the cow-headed woman is the goddess Hathor; the eagle on a staff is his Roman mercenary group.

End of Part I

Synopsis of Part I: Riverland Odyssey (Chapter 1 to 27)

The story begins at Sais, where Captain Muslak has brought Latro after unknown years at Rome. Latro is trying to lift the curse. They take on the job of surveying the upper reaches of the Great River.

The warlock/healer Sahuset helps Latro remember a little bit (6), then nearly kills him in a quest for power that has Latro visit the judges of the dead (9).

Latro gains Uraeus. As they travel up the river, Sahuset's wax woman Sabra becomes more demanding. By chapter 12 she is decidedly vampiric.

At Asyut, Latro honors both the god of jackals and the god of wolves (13–15).

In Wast (Thebes) they get two more jobs, a missing son case and a map to ancient gold mines (18).

They go up the canal around the cataract (23).

Latro and a group head out for the mines (24) but are sidetracked by the god Onuris who gets Latro's help in catching his wife (25).

Latro and the group are prisoners at the mine (26). They escape but Latro and Myt-ser'eu are caught again. Latro is dying.

Part II

28. A Strange Awakening!

28.01: (243–44) Latro wakes up in a sick house where all the men are chained.

28.02: (244) The man on his right does not speak a language Latro knows. Through his pantomime Latro learns that he has been raving mad.

28.03: (244–45) Latro is to be sold as a rower.

28.04: (245) Latro is chained with others and marched all day.

28.05: (245–46) Myt-ser'eu waves and shouts when a ship passes on the river. A guard beats her, so Latro kills him. The owner comes and Myt-ser'eu talks Latro down. Latro takes the place of the guard he killed, and takes up his club.

28.06: (246–47) Latro and Myt-ser'eu are bought by a priest.

28.07: (247–48) The priest is taking them to Meroë, to the last temple. A beetle lands on Latro's chest and stays there.

The priest is Holy Kashta. His god is Seth. The city has four temples, one of Seth, one of Isis, one of Apedemak, and one of the Sun.

Geography: Meroë was the capital of Kush. It was named by the Persian king Cambyses after his sister.

Herodotus: The historian relies on the words of others for his report on Meroë, which he termed "the mother-city of all the other Ethiopians" (Book II):

> 29. From the city of Elephantine as one goes up the river . . . it is a voyage of about four days in length, and in this part the Nile is winding like the river Maiander, and the distance amounts to twelve *schoines*, which one must traverse in this manner. Then you will come to a level plain, in which the Nile flows round an island named Tachompso. . . . After this you will disembark and make a journey by land of forty days; for in the Nile sharp rocks

stand forth out of the water, and there are many reefs, by which it is not possible for a vessel to pass. Then after having passed through this country in the forty days which I have said, you will embark again in another vessel and sail for twelve days; and after this you will come to a great city called Meroe. This city is said to be the mother-city of all the other Ethiopians.

Myth: Apedemak was a lion-headed warrior god, the war god of Kush. To Herodotus, Isis was Demeter and Seth was Typhon.

28.08: (248–49) Myt-ser'eu weeps because they continue to go south, farther from her home in the north by the Great Sea.

Latro feels the last temple is important.

28.09: (249–50) They are in Meroë, housed in the temple of Seth. There are three priests: Kashta, Alara, and Tobarqo.

Latro is to guard the temple at night.

Onomastics: Kashta means "the Kushite."

History: Kashta was king of ancient Nubia (8th century BC), successor of Alara, who founded the dynasty. "Tobarqo" is likely Taharqo (Taharqa or Taharka) the Kushite pharaoh of later times (690–664 BC).

28.10: (250–51) Latro escorts Myt-ser'eu to the market. Half of the houses are in ruins. Talking of the battle they themselves went through, Latro remembers a golden lioness; but Myt-ser'eu says he cannot remember anything.

The royal palace is in ruins. Now the king rules from Napata. Myt-ser'eu says she and Latro were in Napata for a month but Latro was very ill.

At the temple, Latro sets out a dish of milk for the snake. He sees the Moon goddess in the sky.

History: Meroë was ruinous at this point, with the king ruling from Napata. This shift began in the 7th century BC, but Napata declined to the point where the capital moved back to Meroë.

28.11: (251–52) The god speaks to Latro. He says Latro is sleeping, and proves it. The god tells him to carve "lost temple" into his club. He does so.

Comment: The final line "What a strange awakening!" echoes that chapter title, which usually is the first line.

29. We Are Free

29.01: (253–56) The painted king comes and wants to buy Latro. Latro wants him to buy Myt-ser'eu, too.

A brown woman is summoned. She says to Latro she is Queen Bittusilma, and she knows him. He replies in her language. Then the painted king buys both Latro and Myt-ser'eu. Naked as slaves, they leave the temple.

Bittusilma is wife of Seven Lions. She tells Latro, "You and he were great friends long ago."

Bittusilma tells Latro that she and Seven Lions returned to her home in Babylon. They stayed there one year, then they went to his home, where, finding the throne vacant, he took it. Recently a god came to him in a dream, telling him that Latro was in that temple in Meroë. The god told him to take Latro to a certain ruin, far to the south.

Bittusilma wants to go to Babylon, not the ruins. Seven Lions says they will go to Babylon after doing the will of the god.

The beetle stirs, even though it is jewelry.

Myt-ser'eu points out that south is where their ship might be.

The king frees them and gives them clothes. Seven Lions is Mfalme.

Timestamp: That Latro and Seven Lions were great friends "long ago" gives a hint that it has been more than just a few years.

Swahili: Mfalme means "king."

Herodotus: The king is painted red and white, just like our now familiar detail from the army listing: "The Ethiopians had skins of leopards and lions tied upon them. . . . Of their body they used to smear over half with white, when they went into battle, and the other half with red" (Book VII, 69).

29.02: (257) The group passes through a village on the river at the northernmost part of the kingdom. At this place Myt-ser'eu hears that the ship she seeks had passed the day before.

The next day Latro and Myt-ser'eu are in a boat. She gives him a summary of their adventures together and he does not believe it.

Latro meets Unguja, advisor to Seven Lions.

Onomastics: *"Unguja.* Perhaps 'Burned'" (*Sidon* glossary). Unguja is another name for Zanzibar Island.

29.03: (257–58) They are at a village where the river divides into the Blue and the White, the birthplace of Seven Lions. They will follow the White to the ruins they seek.

The king gives information on Latro's life. Latro commanded a hundred soldiers from his city; Mfalme commanded men from his village and others.

Geography: A village located at that spot would be near modern Khartoum, Sudan.

29.04: (258–59) At the village, Latro is on watch at night. He sees the ship glide by and gives chase, but fails to catch it. Returning he finds his fellow sentry, his host, partly eaten by a big dog thing.

It was Latro's fault.

Commentary: This seems hallucinatory. From the text it seems the ship does not usually, if ever, travel by night; and the attacking creature might be natural or supernatural.

29.05: (259–60) Myt-ser'eu binds his wounds from the thorn barrier and they await the judgment of the village.

29.06: (260) The village determines it will be trial by combat.

29.07: (260–61) They stay many days. In the crowd at the fight, Latro sees a small man who seems familiar.

Latro wins the fight and gains another wife, her three children, a hut, and a boat.

The small man says he is Latro's slave, and Myt-ser'eu says this is true. The slave was on a ship but came when he heard Latro's voice.

Commentary: This seems to validate that the ship was real.

30. Rich In Game

30.01: (263–64) The party is in the marshes. They plan to hunt river-horses.

Latro's second wife Cheche shows him the animal that killed the father of her children.

Commentary: The animal seems to be a hyena.

Swahili: Cheche speaks Swahili, giving "simba" for lion, and "chui" for leopard. Cheche means "a baby" (or a small piece; or spark; or a fish with poisonous bones).

30.02: (264–66) They stop at a place to hunt the river-horses. Latro's sons are Vinjari and Utundu. The hunt goes well and the king saves Latro from being trampled.

Latro wants to make a shield, but the king says a god will give him one soon.

Onomastics: Vinjari is Cheche's older son, and his name means "Roamer" (*Sidon* glossary) from a word meaning "browse" or "scout" in Swahili; Utundu is the younger son, and his name means "Mischief" (*Sidon* glossary) from a word meaning "nerve" (mischief, jumpiness, naughtiness).

30.03: (266–67) At the king's city Mji Mkubwa the huts are all on poles because the river floods annually.

Latro reads much of his scroll.

Swahili: "Mji Mkubwa" means "large town."

Commentary: It appears the party is in Nysa now.

30.04: (267) Latro talks with his adopted daughter Binti.

Onomastics: Binti is "daughter" in Swahili.

30.05: (268–69) An unknown number of days later, Latro sits in at the king's court. A girl comes in with a demon problem. Latro wrestles with the demon, and everyone sees it the moment he touches it. Latro kills the demon. The king tells Latro of a time when he touched a greater king of this place and others saw him.

Now the girl attaches herself to Latro's household.

Echo: Seven Lions harkens back to when Latro touched the king of Nysa (*Mist,* Chapter V).

30.06: (269–70) Latro's senior wife tells him to write every day. There are five boats, hollowed from logs. Unguja is in the second boat.

The demon-clawed girl is Mtoto and has become Mytser'eu's servant.

Onomastics: Mtoto is "baby" (or young person; or juvenile) in Swahili. "Probably 'Child'" (*Sidon* glossary).

30.07: (270) At night Latro hears a madman laughing outside the camp. Mvita advises against trying anything, since there are many dangerous animals and demons.

Commentary: The "madman" might be a hyena, or something supernatural.

Onomastics: Mvita is "the water" (or Mombasa) in Swahili.

30.08: (270) During the night Latro sees a large panther that the sentries do not see.

In the morning the women break camp and Latro makes his note.

Commentary: The phantom panther is certainly supernatural.

30.09: (270–71) The party waits at a village for Mzee, a local man who knows the ruins.

Binti cries, fearing that once Latro has restored memory he will go away.

Onomastics: Mzee is "old man" (or respected person; or parent) in Swahili. "Probably 'Elder'" (*Sidon* glossary).

30.10: (271) Mzee returns and the party prepares.

31. In The Bush

31.01: (273–74) They march far from the river, following a dry stream through a deep gorge.

They are camped in a waterless place, one day away from the ruins.

The temple is near. The scarab senses it. The king does not wish to enter it after dark.

31.02: (274) Latro agrees with his senior wife that she may leave him to return to her home. They may see a ship.

31.03: (274) Latro's slave has scouted the temple at night, and says it is a good place.

Latro wonders if there will be trouble with the king.

31.04: (275) Latro tries the sandals Cheche made for him, then he and Myt-ser'eu sleep.

31.05: (275–80) When they set out in the morning, one of the king's warriors is bitten by a snake and dies. Latro's slave goes ahead to make Latro's way safe.

The temple is stone and very old. The king says only he and Latro should enter, but Unguja and Mzee are allowed also. And Latro's two sons.

Once inside, the scarab flies free and indicates a hidden trap door. Latro goes down the stairs alone. The part they had entered was once an upper story.

Latro finds a statue with a cup and a flute. Behind it he finds a small scroll.

Myt-ser'eu appears behind Latro on the stairs, and a black man with burning eyes behind her. She says Latro promised to give the scroll to Sahuset.

Latro tries to open it, then puts it away. The other man has vanished.

Together Latro and Myt-ser'eu go down the second stair. In the holiest place they find the rude statue of a woman. One hand has a cross, the other holds an arrow. Her headdress is a disk.

Myt-ser'eu prays. The goddess steps forward and grants her prayers, the one spoken and the one unspoken.

The promised shield is there.

Back up on the surface, Latro's son Vinjari spears a snake that turns into a man.

It is Latro's slave, who dies in his arms. They try to bury him, but the body disappears. Vinjari walks off. Latro tracks him a long way, but then loses the trail.

Vinjari is gone. Latro has the shield the goddess gave.

Myth: The single arrow and the shield are signs of the goddess Hemuset.

Commentary: Latro has accomplished the prophecy of the scroll from the temple of the wolf god.

31.06: (280–81) Polishing the shield, Latro sees moving images of his younger self throwing his sword into the river. And Latro gains this memory.

Commentary: That he sees his life in the shield proves the truth of the legend.

32. The Queen Is Overjoyed

32.01: (283–84) They will go down the Great River the next day. Latro talks with the king, who tells him many things they saw together in Hellas. Latro tells of his quest for the lost sword. It must be in Nubia. The king and queen will go, too.

Already the things Seven Lions told him are fading.

Onomastics: As a reverse-translation exercise, "Seven Lions" in Swahili is "simba saba." This leads to "Saba Simba," the stage name/persona of an American professional wrestler for one year (1990–1991). Was the wrestler himself, or someone with influence over him, a fan of Latro?

32.02: (284–86) Myt-ser'eu is furious about this new sword quest.

32.03: (286–87) The ship arrives. Latro hands over the small scroll to Sahuset. They will take Myt-ser'eu home.

32.04: (287–88) Qanju says this group thought Latro and Myt-ser'eu were dead. They sailed up the Blue, then sailed up the White.
   Commentary: It seems that, aside from the three bowmen who died, all the others at the mine got away: Sabra, Uraeus, Holy Thotmaktef, Alala, Neht-nefret, the prisoners Kames and Prince Nasakhma.

32.05: (288) They have a big party with lots of pombe, but Latro is sad to be parting from Myt-ser'eu.
   Commentary: In central and eastern Africa, pombe is a fermented drink made from grains and fruit.

32.06: (288–89) A woman with a great cat is searching among the sleepers. The queen is drunk, and propositions Latro, but he declines. He wonders if she is the one the tall woman seeks.

32.07: (289–90) Latro at watch on the ship meets Sahuset's wife. She says she needs the queen's blood. She says she will be Latro's new wife when his wife soon leaves him.

32.08: (290) The queen Bittusilma talks with Latro. She has a wound on her arm and says she got it at the party.

33. Our Whole Company

33.01: (291–93) Latro discusses his sword quest with all on the ship. The captain mentions that this trip from Sais has been many months.

33.02: (293–94) While in the reeds with Holy Thotmaktef, Latro sees the fair-haired huntress escorting the priest's baboon through the air. From her side she draws the arrow that had dyed her gown with her own blood.
   Commentary: This is a highly charged, enigmatic moment. At the level of Latro's personal life, it seems a vision of his great love the red-haired Amazon who died from an arrow, but of course he cannot remember that. It seems the goddess of the lost temple has been freed by Latro's presence and action, and

now she goes to join others. She seems to be Mehit, as rescued by Onuris, or as an Eye of Ra rescued by a god.

33.03: (294–97) In the night, Qanju gives Latro notes on his future. "For years you will walk in a circle, following the path left by your own feet."

Next in the night, Sabra talks to Latro. At long last she gets him to remove Myt-ser'eu's amulet.

At sunrise Latro sees a boat bring the sun, and the baboon rides in its prow.

33.04: (297–98) The queen was sliced in the night. Now the men nail Sabra's box shut.

The episode has alienated the king from Latro.

33.05: (298) They are at Naqa in Nubia.

Geography: Naqa is a ruined city in modern Sudan. One of the centers of the kingdom Meroë, it was a trading station on the way east from the Nile. It had temples to Amun and Apedemak.

34. I Am Alone

34.01: (299–301) They do not find Falcata in Naqa.

At the inn Latro is awakened from sleep. He sees a man holding Falcata. Aided by the baboon, Latro gives chase. When the sun comes up, he finds his way back to the inn. Myt-ser'eu is gone, having left with a smaller foreign man. She had tried to take the shield and spear.

The ship is gone.

Latro will buy a boat the next day.

Commentary: It looks like Latro and Myt-ser'eu were separated through a two-messages trick, wherein Latro followed a vision and Myt-ser'eu was led to believe he was already at the ship.

34.02: (301) Latro is ill, forced to write by someone.

34.03: (301–302) It is nearly noon. The night before he was sick.

He saw a woman who burned. The baboon is around, it seems.
He will arise and walk.

34.04: (302) Latro is found on the road by Medjays.

34.05: (302–304) Latro tells the chief about the woman who burned. The chief will give him a horse the next day.

Commentary: That the woman burned implies that Sabra killed Sahuset and was obliterated by Beteshu, fulfilling his vow.

34.06: (304) Latro tracks the horse all day. It is brown.

34.07: (304–305) The goddesss Mehit helps Latro.

34.08: (305) Latro rides north on Ater his horse. The horse came to him because of lions.

Onomastics: In Latin, "ater" is "black, dark."

34.09: (305–306) Latro has only the baboon for company.

34.10: (306) The baboon leaves while Latro reads. Now he is alone.

35. Two

35.01: (307–10) Latro polishes his shield at night and remembers a white stallion of the sun.

At the river Latro sets Ater free. Then he makes like a madman with the boatman, claiming to have murdered his wife, their children, his parents, and his in-laws.

He goes to the city on the island in the river. People tell him the ship passed three days before. At a temple of Isis he prays. He offers to serve her.

The goddess speaks to him, giving instructions: "[W]alk toward the north star until you find your sword. Turn your steps then toward the rising sun." She assures him he has no blood guilt.

Commentary: Herodotus sees Isis as Demeter.

35.02: (310–11) Latro returns to the temple of Seth where he had once been a slave. He spends the night there.

Commentary: So Latro is in Meroë again.

35.03: (311–12) The watchmen tell Latro that during the night a woman came with her maid, looking for her husband. At that time a dog ran into the temple, and they ask Latro to help them find it. Latro uses food to get the dog out.

Now he has a dog.

35.04: (312) Cautus's barking wakes Latro. The baboon directs him to write. It seems that Mtoto the scarred child and Myt-ser'eu have found Latro and will help him search for Falcata.

Onomastics: "Cautus" means "Watchful." "This name may be a pun on canis, 'dog'" (*Sidon* glossary).

THE END

Synopsis of Part II: Into Nysa and Back Again (Chapter 28 to 35)

Latro begins writing again in a sick house for slaves. He and Myt-ser'eu are sold to a priest who takes them south to his temple of Seth in Meroë.

Latro and Myt-ser'eu are purchased by the painted king, who turns out to be Seven Lions, still married to Bittusilma. A god told Seven Lions to buy Latro and take him to a certain ruin far to the south.

Along the way at a village there is a complication that gives Latro another wife and her children, as well as the return of his servant Uraeus (29).

They have a river-horse hunting party.

Latro cures a girl of demonic possession and gains another follower.

They arrive at the ruin. Latro finds a scroll that he had promised for Sahuset. Then he an Myt-ser'eu meet the goddess and get the shield. But Latro's son Vinjari kills Uraeus.

They head down the river. Now Latro wants to find his sword in Nubia (32). He sees the phantom baboon leading a fair-haired goddess away (33).

They fail to find Falcata in Naqa, and Latro is separated from the rest. He becomes ill, physically and mentally. He prays to Isis and she advises him. He works at the Temple of Seth and Myt-ser'eu finds him there.

APPENDICES FOR SOLDIER OF SIDON

Appendix L3-1: Preliminary Notes

Sir Richard Francis Burton has the dedication in *Soldier of Sidon*, celebrated for his achievements in exploration and translating.

Sir Richard explored a number of places, but his exploration of the Great Lakes of Africa (1856–60) was part of the Search for the Source of the Nile, which is similar to Latro's job. He wrote many books, among them a translation of *The Book of the Thousand Nights and a Night* (1885) that was a literary milestone.

Technically, Sir Richard's travels did not take him up the Nile; rather, he cut across from Zanzibar. His adventures in the swamps seem to influence Latro's time in Nysa.

The Arabian Nights seems translated into the sorcery and the pagan gods, the ghosts and monsters, of Latro's Egyptian adventure. The wax woman, a spooky wax golem with vampiric hunger, seems especially like something from the Arabian Nights.

Another strange similarity is in the adventure fiction *King Solomon's Mines* (1885), a novel by another that draws upon Sir Richard's African exploration and was published in the same year as Sir Richard's translation of the Arabian Nights. This has bearing on Latro's tale in his search for the lost gold mines, first mentioned in Chapter 18, then acted upon in Chapters 24 to 27.

In *Sidon*, Herodotus continues to have a large impact on Latro's narrative. The historian claimed to have visited Egypt, where he traveled up the Nile as far as Elephantine. Again, there is travel and investigation. There are those who claim Herodotus never visited Egypt. Again, there is the tension between fact and fiction.

Considering The Latro Novels As A Whole

Latro's scrolls are divided into ten "parts," listed here with the brief descriptions used previously.

1. From Clay to the Lady of Dawn
2. From meeting Hypereides to meeting the Maiden
3. From Kalleos to Rope
4. From Acheron to Sestos
5. From Sestos to Pactye
6. The Apsinthian Labor
7. From Thought to Rope
8. From the Oracle to the Games
9. Riverland Odyssey
10. Into Nysa and Back Again

The Tone Of Each Latro Novel

Soldier of the Mist strikes me as having a lot of moon imagery. The lunar phases help track the passage of time, and the phases are important for showing the nature of the three-person moon goddess as linking to the New Moon, the Crescent Moon, and the Full Moon. There is also the breezy mystery of the moonlit Dionysian orgy at the lake. While things get rough, there is always a certain optimistic quality.

In contrast, *Soldier of Arete* is very grim. It seems to be Latro's "book of war," even though half of it involves the athletics of the games.

Soldier of Sidon seems like the book of magic and madness. Latro definitely travels along the shaman path: his essence is broken into five parts; he visits the judging gods; he suffers fits of madness.

In short, the Latro novels are Monday, Tuesday, and Wednesday.

Appendix L3-2: The Latro Of Sidon

King Seven Lions tells Latro he was a leader of one hundred, so he was a centurion, as mentioned by a person at the mines.

In addition, Maluk says that Latro had missed the boat from Egypt and had to march all the way to Sidon, presumably from Mennufer (Memphis). This seems like an epic journey, after which he hired on as a soldier of Sidon. But Sidon was famous for supplying ships and sailors; the army list does not mention Sidon or Phoenicians providing land forces.

Latro's return to Rome, in the years between *Arete* and *Sidon*, allows the possibility for him to be a prototype for the velites, the future light infantry of the Roman army.

Latro And The Gods Of Egypt

Latro's adventure resolves cleanly as a Return of the Eye of Ra, wherein a goddess runs away from her father Ra, who sends one of the gods to retrieve her. Latro assists Thoth in getting Hemuset.

The god Set is scary, but his sorcerer is more of a problem, and the sorcerer's creature Sabra is the worst.

Latro's Powers

Appendix L2-2 discusses the powers of Latro (spirit sight, spirit reveal, temporary resurrection, and Nike) but there are also temporary "perfume" powers granted to Latro through divine particles or pollen. This is a different angle on the "divinity as disease" model mentioned twice in the novels (*Arete* Ch. 4; *Sidon* Ch. 6).

The most vivid example is the one that gives the "pollen" name to the model: the tryst in the flower between Latro and Aphrodite (*Mist,* Ch. XX). After this experience Latro is propositioned by Kalleos, which implies that the pollen of the love goddess gave Latro a love perfume.

This model might also explain some details around the Kid celebration that takes place offstage between chapter III and IV of *Mist.* In a much later chapter, the Huntress mentions that she had been searching for Dionysus that dawn but she found Latro instead, suggestive of a Dionysus perfume on the mortal. Hilaeira, after being intimate with Latro at the celebration, becomes "religious" to the point of being guaranteed the highest position at the Eleusian temple before she has even become an initiate, another tangible trace of the perfume.

In *Arete,* Latro's proximity in sleeping near the Thracian Rider grants him such an aroma of arete that first the Amazons notice it in a positive way, and then the Thracians detect it in a negative way.

Note that these cases are not possessions by the gods: Latro is not Dionysus, nor Aphrodite, nor Ares. Latro is not displaced from his body as Eurykles is displaced by Drakaina. The perfume effect is of relatively short duration.

Contrary to this pattern is a case of divine contact where Latro experiences no perfume effect: the episode where he wakes up in the field with his head being cradled in the hands of the god Arensnuphis. Latro subsequently goes on a mission with this god to capture the goddess Mehit, but he does not seem to get any perfume out of it. He does get direct favors from the goddess Mehit, so maybe that is the distinction.

Another power that is not a possession is the vehicle mode used by the phantom boar from *Mist* to *Arete.* In *Sidon* there are a few instances where this might happen: in one he takes in a personal demon to help him with his memory; in another he accidentally gets a bit of Osiris blood; a third is the episode with Arensnuphis. Later on, after the escape from the gold mine, he spends a month as a raving madman. While this episode of madness could be a psychological reaction to the traumas he suffered at the mines, it could also be an expression of multiple entities possessing his body, or these entities all leaving his body.

So perhaps Latro himself has become a "solar boat" onto which loaded a lot of other gods.

Latro's Future

Isis says Latro will find his sword in the north, then he will go east (310).

Sahuset says Myt-ser'eu will return to her native place, and leave it again (89).

Putting these together, it seems likely that they will travel north to Sais, find the sword along the way, and then together go east. While Maluk has offered Latro a ride to Sidon, he will likely chose to walk.

Appendix L3-3: Timelines

Sais: See healer, buy river wives (chapters 1, 2) 1 day

<break>

ship/inn: First inn (chapter 3) 1 day

<break>

ship: Sleep on ship (chapter 4) 1 day
ship: Inn at Mennufer (chapter 4) 1 day
Mennufer: Cosmetics, White Wall, spell (chapters 4–6) 1 day
Mennufer/ship/village: Mystery of 3rd woman (chapter 7) 1 day
ship/village: Death and revival (chapters 8–10) 1 day

<break>

ship (chapters 11, 12) 1 day

<break?>

ship/Asyut (chapters 13, 14) 1 day
Asyut: Morning bullfighting, procession (chapter 14) 1 day
Asyut: Night at necropolis, then inn (chapter 14) 1 day
Asyut/ship/Wast: Sacrifice, travel, inn (chapters 15–17) 1 day
Wast: Buy wine and water, gain Agathocles (chapter 18) 1 day
ship/town: Latro waits for the Red One (chapter 19) 1 day
ship/Abu: Slept through most of day (chapter 20–22.02) 1 day
Abu: Washer-woman quest (chapter 22.03) 1 day
Abu (chapter 23.01–.02) 1 day
canal (chapter 23.03) 1 day

<break> (3 days?)

town (chapter 24.01–.02) 1 day
town/horses: Setting out east (chapter 24.03–25.02) 1 day
Red Land: Wake up with Onuris (chapter 25.03–.04) 1 day

with Onuris: Task with Onuris (chapter 25.05–.06) 1 day

<break>

gold mine (chapter 26) 1 day

<break?>

country: Recapture (chapter 27) 1 day

<break> (more than a month)

Napata: Slave pen (chapter 28.01–.04) 1 day

<break>

road: Latro kills guard, becomes guard (chapter 28.05) 1 day

<break>

road: Priest is new owner (chapter 28.06) 1 day

<break>

road: Cataract (chapter 28.07) 1 day

<break>

road: Continuing south (chapter 28.08) 1 day

<break>

Meroë (chapter 28.09) 1 day

<break?>

Meroë: Walk through ruins (chapter 28.10–.11) 1 day
Meroë/ship: Bought and freed (chapter 29.01) 1 day
ship/village (chapter 29.02) 1 day
ship/village: River divides (chapter 29.03–.04) 1 day
village: Trouble (chapter 29.05–.07) 4 day

<break>

marshes: Hippo hunt (chapter 30.01–.02) 1 day

\<break\>

Mji Mkubwa: Wrestles demon (chapter 30.03–.04) 1 day

\<break\>

boat: Five boats (chapter 30.06–.08) 1 day

\<break\>

village (chapter 30.09–.10) 2 day

\<break\>

bush (chapter 31.01–.04) 1 day
temple (chapter 31.05) 1 day
bush: Polishing shield (chapter 31.06) 1 day

\<break\>

river side: Rest, reunion, feast (chapter 32.01–.06) 1 day
ship (chapter 32.07–.08, 33.01–.03) 1 day
ship (chapter 33.04) 1 day

\<break?\>

Naqa (chapter 33.05) 1 day
Naqa (chapter 34.01) 1 day
road: Sick (chapter 34.02) 1 day
road: Vision of the woman burning (chapter 34.03–.05) 1 day
country: Tracking the horse (chapter 34.06) 1 day
country: Help from Mehit (chapter 34.07) 1 day
country: Riding north (chapter 34.08–.10) 1 day
Meroë (chapter 35.01–.02) 1 day
Meroë (chapter 35.03–.04) 1 day

L3-4: Apollo Prophecy Checklist (Number 3)

Latro is taken to a temple of Apollo (*Mist,* chapter III), where the god says to him, "Only the solitary may see the gods. For the rest, every god is the Unknown God" (11). After a bit of conversation, Apollo says:

> A. "I prophesy that though you will wander far in search of your home, you will not find it until you are farthest from it.
>
> B. Once only, you will sing as men sang in the Age of Gold to the playing of the gods.
>
> C. Long after, you will find what you seek in the dead city.
>
> D. "Though healing is mine, I cannot heal you, nor would I if I could; by the shrine of the Great Mother you fell, to a shrine of hers you must return.
>
> E. Then she will point the way, and in the end the wolf's tooth will return to her who sent it
>
> F. Look beneath the sun...." (11–12).

The version of the pythoness goes:
    1. Look under the sun, if you would see!
    2. Sing! Make sacrifice to me!
    3. But you must cross the narrow sea.
    4. The wolf that howls has wrought you woe!
    5. To that dog's mistress you must go!
    6. Her hearth burns in the room below.
    7. I send you to the God Unseen!
    8. Whose temple lies in Death's terrene!
    9. There you shall learn why He's not seen.
    10. Sing then, and make the hills resound!
    11. King, nymph, and priest shall gather round!
    12. Wolf, faun, and nymph, spellbound. (15)

The Apollo and Pythoness lines seem related at points:

A/Pythoness
A
B/2, 10–11
C
D/5
E/6
F/1

Most of the lines seem fulfilled:

A (Chapter fulfilled in Mist)
A
B (V: king of Nysa, nymph Hilaeira, priest Pindaros)
C
D (XIX: meet the Maiden)
E (XIX: meet the Maiden)
F

P (Chapter fulfilled in Arete)
3 (7: cross narrow sea)
12 (41: wolf Latro, faun Aglaus, and nymph Elata)
1 (32: Cybele says, Look under the sun)

A (Chapter fulfilled in Sidon)
C (14: dead city, where Latro gains scarab pendant)

L3-5: Latro And The Gods (3)

A list of supernatural details.

- Meet goddess Hathor (ch. 2)
- The memory xu (ch. 6)
- Meet Sesostris (ch. 10)
- See wolf-headed god (ch. 14)
- Meet the All-Beast (ch. 17)
- Meet Beteshu (ch. 21)
- Beteshu's warning to Sabra (ch. 22)
- Meet god Arensnuphis (ch. 24)
- God in dream to Seven Lions (ch. 29)
- Wrestles demon at court (ch. 30)
- Meet goddess Hemuset (ch. 31)
- See Hemuset with baboon (ch. 33)
- Vision of man with Falcata; vision of woman who burned (ch. 34)
- Help from goddess Mehit (ch. 34)
- Meet goddess Isis (ch. 35)

Appendix L3-6: Lives Circa 469 Before Christ, And After

Achaemenes—Brother of Xerxes, he became Satrap of Egypt after the rebellion against Persian rule circa 485 BC. He survived the Battle of Salamis (480 BC). In 460 BC, Egypt revolted. Achaemenes met the native prince Inaros in the Battle of Papremis (459 BC) where the Persian was defeated and slain.

Artabazos—Persian general in the army of Xerxes, he withdrew his forces from the Battle of Plataea (479 BC) and led his remnant of the army out of Greece and back to Ionia. As a reward he was made satrap of Hellespontine Phrygia, and became first of a dynasty there.

Cimon—Celebrated hero of the Battle of Salamis (480 BC). He destroyed the Persian fleet and army at the Battle of the Eurymedon river (466 BC). He led an unsuccessful expedition to support the Spartans during the helot uprisings of 462 BC; for which failure he was dismissed and ostracized from Athens (461 BC); only to be recalled from his ten-year exile to negotiate a five-year treaty between Sparta and Athens (451 BC). Died in Cyprus 449 BC.

Gorgo (Queen)—Daughter of King Cleomenes (whose ghost was raised at Acheron (*Mist,* chapter XXXIII)), wife of her uncle King Leonides (whom Latro fought at Thermopylae (*Mist,* chapter XXXVII)), and mother of King Pleistarchus.

Hegesistratus—Caught by Spartans while practicing divination on the island Zakynthos, he was put to death. Presumably this is soon after the end of *Arete.*

Nasakhma—Kushite King of Meroë, he reigned between Siaspiqa and Malewiebamani. He was buried at Nuri.

Pausanias—Spartan hero of the Battle of Palatea (479 BC). In 478 BC he was recalled to Sparta on suspicion of conspiring with the Persians. Then he went to Byzantium and conspired with the Persians. He returned to Sparta and was rumored to have offered to free helots for an uprising. He was executed by starvation circa 470 BC.

Pericles—Greek statesman whose name marks the "Age of Pericles" (461 to 429 BC) a high point of Greek civilization. He ostracized Cimon in 461 BC. He died during the Plague of Athens in 429 BC.

Pindaros—Theban poet, one of the canonical nine lyric poets of ancient Greece. He visited Sicily in 476–75 BC. He composed his first Pythian ode in 470 BC, writing on the topic of the victories at Salamis and Plataea. He died circa 438 BC.

Pleistarchus—King of Sparta 480 BC to his death in 458 BC.

Simonides—Simonides of Ceos, another one of the canonical nine lyric poets of ancient Greece. The celebrated poet and mnemonicist returned to Athens from Thessaly during the Persian Wars. His last years were in Sicily, and he died circa 468 BC.

Themistocles—Athenian politician and general. He fought at the Battle of Marathon (490 BC). He pushed for the buildup of the Athenian Navy, which then saw victory at Salamis (480 BC). He directed the rebuilding of Athens. Spartans tied him to the alleged treason of their own Pausanias, and around 471 BC Themistocles fled Greece. Eventually he served the Persian king as governor of Magnesia, where he died in 459 BC.

Xanthippus—His rivalry with Themistocles led to his ostracism, but he was recalled from exile when the Persians invaded Greece. He was in command at the Battle of Mycale. He was at the Siege of Sestus. He returned to Athens a hero, but he died a few years later. His son was Pericles.

Xerxes—The fourth King of Kings, he was assassinated by court plotters in 465 BC.

BIBLIOGRAPHY

Anonymous. "Homeric Hymn to Dionysus."
———. "Homeric Hymn 16."
Aramini, Marc. *Beyond Time and Memory*. 2020.
Athenaeus. *The Learned Banqueters.*
Bauscher, David. *English-Aramaic and Aramaic-English Dictionary.* 2008.
Budge, E. A. Wallis. *Literature of the Ancient Egyptians.*
———. *The Papyrus of Ani.*
Crampton, Jeremy. "Some Greek Themes in Gene Wolfe's Latro novels." Ultan's Library, 2000.
Dante (translated by Sibbald). *The Divine Comedy.*
Dunsany. "The Exiles Club." 1916.
Durr, Kay. *Ancient Egyptian Names for Dogs.* Alpine Publications, 1996.
Eliade, Mircea. *Zalmoxis: The Vanishing God.* 1970.
Gray, Harold. *Little Orphan Annie.* Beginning 1924.
Haggard, H. Rider. *King Solomon's Mines.* 1885.
Herodas. "Mime 6" and "Mime 7."
Herodotus (translated by G. C. Macaulay). *The Histories.*
———. (translated by George Rawlinson).
———. (translated by A. D. Godley).
Homer. *The Iliad.*
———. *The Odyssey.*
Pausanias (geographer). *Description of Greece.* Circa AD 150.
Petronius. *Satyricon.*
Pindaros. "First Pythian Ode."
———. "Olympian I."
———. "Olympian II."
———. Dithyrambs, Fragment 78.

———. Fragment of a Dithyramb, to be sung at Athens.
Plato. *Symposium*. Circa 380 BC.
Pliny the Elder. *Natural History*.
Poe, Edgar Allan. "Murders in the Rue Morgue." 1841.
Rosenthal, Franz (ed.). *An Aramaic Handbook*. Otto Harrassowitz, Wiesbaden. 1967.
Simonides of Ceos. Poems at Thermopylae.
Smith, William. *Dictionary of Greek and Roman Geography*.
Thucydides (translated by Richard Crawley). *The History of the Peloponnesian War*.
Wolfe, Gene. *Castle of Days*.
Xenophon. *Symposium*. Circa 368 BC.

BOOKS BY THIS AUTHOR

Gene Wolfe's The Book Of The New Sun: A Chapter Guide

A chapter-by-chapter guide to Gene Wolfe's "The Book of the New Sun," its sequel "The Urth of the New Sun," and four shorter works.

Gene Wolfe's First Four Novels: A Chapter Guide

A chapter guide to Gene Wolfe's early novels "Operation ARES" (1970), "The Fifth Head of Cerberus" (1972), "Peace" (1975), and "The Devil in a Forest" (1976).

Gene Wolfe: 14 Articles On His Fiction

Ten essays and four reviews, originally published from 1993 to 2014, in "The New York Review of Science Fiction," "Foundation," "Extrapolation," "Ultan's Library," "The Magazine of Fantasy & Science Fiction," "The Internet Review of Science Fiction," "Quantum," and a chapbook on "The Fifth Head of Cerberus." Some of them are available for free online, but many are hard to find.

Roadside Picnic Revisited: Seven Articles On The Soviet Novel That Inspired The Film "Stalker"

A collection of essays and a book review relating to "Roadside

Picnic," the Soviet science fiction novel by Arkady and Boris Strugatsky. Six of the pieces were originally published in "The New York Review of Science Fiction," and the seventh is previously unpublished. The subject is the novel, and there is nothing about the movie "Stalker" beyond a brief mention.

Printed in Great Britain
by Amazon